Kathrin Fäller

"And it's all there" – Intertextual Structures, Themes, and Characters in Stephenie Meyer's "Twilight" Series

D1823585

Kathrin Fäller

"And it's all there" – Intertextual Structures, Themes, and Characters
in Stephenie Meyer's "Twilight" Series

GRIN Verlag

Bibliografische Information der Deutschen Nationalbibliothek: Die Deutsche Bibliothek
verzeichnet diese Publikation in der Deutschen Nationalbibliografie; detaillierte bibliografische Daten sind im Internet über http://dnb.d-nb.de/ abrufbar.

1. Auflage 2010
Copyright © 2010 GRIN Verlag GmbH
http://www.grin.com
Druck und Bindung: Books on Demand GmbH, Norderstedt Germany
ISBN 978-3-656-06624-8

Martin-Luther-Universität Halle-Wittenberg

Philosophische Fakultät II
Philologien, Kommunikations- und Musikwissenschaften
Institut für Anglistik und Amerikanistik

Diplomarbeit

"And it's all there" – Intertextual Structures, Themes, and Characters in Stephenie Meyer's *Twilight* Series

Vorgelegt von: Kathrin Fäller

Datum der Abgabe: 4.11.2010

Table of Contents

1. Introduction

> I know the exact date of my dream – it was June 2, 2003 [...] I woke up that morning with a dream fresh in my head. The dream was vivid, strong, colorful... It was a conversation between a boy and a girl which took place in a beautiful, sunny meadow in the middle of a dark forest. The boy and the girl were in love with each other, and they were discussing the problems involved with that love, seeing that she was human and he was a vampire. The boy was more beautiful than the meadow, and his skin sparkled like diamonds in the sun. He was gentle and polite, and yet the potential for violence was very strong, inherent to the scene. I delayed getting out of bed for a while [...] Finally, I had to get up [...] I sat down at the computer and started writing it out.[1]

Stephenie Meyer, whose debut novel *Twilight* was published in 2005 and hit bestseller lists within a few weeks of its release, devised the idea for her first book in a dream that later became one of the central scenes of her first novel. Similarly, it was Mary Shelley who in her 1831 introduction to *Frankenstein* tells the reader about a waking dream in which she witnesses Frankenstein's creation of the monster. Her nightmare and the subsequent decision that "what terrified me will terrify others"[2] served as the catalyst for the conception of one of the most influential Gothic novels ever written. Eventually, the dream she had on June 16, 1816 became known as "the most famous dream in literary history"[3].

As a postmodern work within the realm of fantastic literature, Meyer situates her tetralogy within a tradition of vampire literature that spans back more than two hundred years. Over the centuries the vampire has proven to be an intensely multi-faceted creature with an inherent capability to represent the fears and longings of individuals and the society in which it dwells. Inspired by Goethe's *Die Braut von Korinth* which shows a young undead girl craving for the love of her predetermined husband a number of Romantic writers composed poems following Goethe's depiction of the vampiric girl. With the delineation of female passionate vampires and fatal women in the poems of Coleridge and Keats groundwork was efficiently laid for representations of vampiresses ranging from determinedly friendship-seeking and intimate to overtly voluptuous seductresses.

Similarly, through Polidori's portrayal of the male aristocratic revenant seducing men as well as women and arousing intimacy but eventually denying it, a portrait of a vampire is

---

[1] Stephenie Meyer on the genesis of her first *Twilight* novel: Stephenie Meyer, "Interview: 'Twilight' author Stephanie [sic] Meyer," Interview with Wm Morris, *A Motley Vision: Mormon Arts and Culture* 26 Oct. 2005, 1 Nov. 2010 <http://www.motleyvision.org/2005/interview-twilight-author-stephanie-meyer/>.
[2] Mary Shelley, "Introduction to 'Frankenstein', Third Edition (1831)," in Mary Shelley, *Frankenstein*, ed. J. Paul Hunter (New York, London: W.W. Norton & Company, 1996) 172.
[3] Anne K. Mellor, *Mary Shelley: Her Life, her Fiction, her Monsters* (London: Routledge, 1989) 37.

3

crafted which efficiently illustrates notions of power and alienation at the heart of society. Epitomized in Stoker's *Dracula* which allegorizes the twentieth-century prototype of the male vampire as a well-groomed but essentially evil other, a type of vampire eventually emerges that turns particularly sympathetic in the course of the years by means of its Romantic predecessors. Due to a change in perspective – a narration from within rather than from outside of the monster – and the consequential "domestication" or humanization of the undead, the vampire in contemporary literature becomes more and more like the humans who face it. Being no longer a clear-cut other but transforming itself into a version of ourselves, the vampire no longer serves as a representative of relatively uncomplicated evil. As formerly established boundaries blur and concepts of good and evil disintegrate its metaphorical charge similarly shifts. Creating a net of coded reflections, the vampire more than ever can tell us something about love and sexuality, power and alienation as well as illness in a postmodern cultural framework.

With the growth in popularity due to series like Anne Rice's *The Vampire Chronicles* and the motif's recurring presence in cinematic adaptations of Stoker's *Dracula* as well as various TV formats public interest has never ceased to the present day. Moreover, Stephenie Meyer's *Twilight* series has in fact accelerated the entire genre of vampire fiction leading to grand popularity and the exploitation of the genre within the realm of popular culture. As the most significant characteristic of the vampire is its being multi-faceted and changing, its potential to be also of great intertextual value can be thereupon considered. Consequently, it can be assumed that Meyer's tetralogy clearly evokes these instances of intertextuality through the adoption of patterns and themes that have already proved productive in earlier literary works. However, in Meyer's work these sources are remarkably extended and sometimes even altered as she relies to a large part on her pretexts to tell her narrative and construct a postmodern vampire figure. The author herself is also aware of her work's intertextual potential as she notes that "it's all there"[4] in earlier literary works. As Meyer's texts take part in a phenomenon that is fairly recent the intertextual potential of vampire literature and of Meyer's works in particular has not yet been explored.

In order to achieve a comprehensive analysis it is necessary to incorporate all four volumes – *Twilight, New Moon, Eclipse,* and *Breaking Dawn* – of the *Twilight* series in the discussion. Meyer's just recently published work *The Short Second Life of Bree Tanner: An*

---

[4] "An Interview with Stephenie Meyer" (supplementary material on 2nd DVD). *Twilight: Biss zum Morgengrauen,* dir. Catherine Hardwicke, perfs. Robert Pattinson, Kristen Stewart, and Billy Burke, 2008, DVD, 2 Disc Fan Edition, Concorde Home Entertainment, 2009.

Eclipse Novella will only engage a marginal part of the analysis as it largely concentrates on the subplot of *Eclipse*, hence not being particularly significant for the main events of the story. On the other hand, Meyer's *Midnight Sun*, although until the present day a yet unfinished and unpublished manuscript, is of great importance for the subsequent analysis. As it narrates the events of Meyer's debut novel *Twilight* from Edward Cullen's point of view it is essential to the understanding of the vampire's perspective. It can be considered a valid and relevant part of the series even though it is not widely read among the general readership of Meyer's novels.

In my diploma thesis, I will trace back the sources Stephenie Meyer employs in her *Twilight* tetralogy regarding structures, themes, and characters. I will point out how they are adopted throughout her novels and in how far they influence the characteristics of Meyer's work. Through that the question arises to what extent Meyer adopts the means of intertextuality to compose her stories. Therefore, questions to be considered are: What pretexts serve as structural layers for Meyer's tetralogy? Does Meyer create an intertextual paradigm that can be found throughout her entire work? Are pretextual references distinctly marked within the series through direct quotations, allusions or by rather covert means of reference such as stereotypes? Are they obvious to the common reader? Are implicit intertextual references apparent to author and reader? Does Meyer employ intertextual markers in the paratext of her works? How far are intertextual markers contextualized in the themes of *Twilight*? How does Meyer handle already prominent motifs? What is the relation between the ideas in intertexts and pretexts – are they in agreement or do they contradict each other? Which role does interfigurality play in Meyer's tetralogy? How do Meyer's characters deal with their interfigurality? Do they have the capacity to reflect on it? What can the names of Meyer's characters tell us and where do they come from? Which forms do pretexts take in the tetralogy? Are they simply referred to or can they form a physical part of the world Meyer created? Are there any references to entire literary genres in Meyer's work? What is the nature of the pretexts Meyer relies on? Which genres do they adhere to?

Meyer dwells on a number of themes, structures, and characters that have intertextual potential. One can distinguish between pretexts that are apparently marked in Meyer's work and sources that only bear non-literal intertextual references. Pretexts that are overtly marked and are thus explicitly intertextual in the *Twilight* series are: Emily Brontë's *Wuthering Heights*, William Shakespeare's *Romeo and Juliet*, *The Midsummer Night's Dream* and *The Merchant of Venice*, Bram Stoker's *Dracula* as well as Jane Austen's *Pride and Prejudice*,

5

Sense and Sensibility and *Mansfield Park*. A number of other pretexts are only covertly marked as they point back to literary traditions or character types. Pretexts that are implicitly marked are: Mary Shelley's *Frankenstein*, Johann Wolfgang von Goethe's *Die Braut von Korinth*, Samuel Taylor Coleridge's *The Rime of the Ancient Mariner* and *Christabel*, John Keats' *Lamia*, Henry Mackenzie's *The Man of Feeling*, Lord Byron's *Manfred* as well as Roman Polanski's movie adaptation of *Rosemary's Baby*.

To answer the questions which have been pointed out so far I will proceed as follows: An overview of the concept of hermeneutic, structuralist intertextuality as well as interfigurality (chapter 2.1.) is first of all necessary as pretextual references in Meyer's work range widely from overt intertextual markers such as direct quotations to covert references. This approach focuses more on description and systemization in order to analyze two or more interrelated literary works. These implicit references to pretexts refer to certain character types as the anti-mother, damsel in distress and the *femme fatale* or to a heroic tradition like the Byronic hero. Since Meyer adopts different point of views in her tetralogy and especially endows her themes, motifs, and symbols with intertextual potential it is also beneficial to begin with a closer look on the narrator as well as themes, motifs, and symbols (chapter 2.2.). Meyer situates her novels within a twenty-first-century framework displaying vampires that have the potential to be good as well as evil, thus making it necessary to place her work within the context of contemporary vampire fiction (chapter 3.1.). A look at present-day research on the *Twilight* saga will also be beneficial to support the *raison d'être* of the analysis at hand (chapter 3.2.). *Twilight*'s vampiric protagonist, Edward Cullen, is placed within the tradition of the Byronic hero, thus incorporating characteristics from this hero type as well as the preceding Man of Feeling. As such it is of great relevance to take a closer look at the eighteenth- and nineteenth-century heroic tradition (chapter 4.1.-2.). Moreover, Meyer borrows a number of characteristics from the nineteenth-century vampire, who also inherited qualities from the Byronic hero, in her portrayal of the male and female vampires in her series (chapter 4.3.).

Meyer's depiction of the postmodern vampire figure (chapter 5.1.) is intertextually productive as she constructs her vampires on the basis of their nineteenth-century predecessors, thus relying on the motif of the *femme fatale* as well as the Byronic hero. The distinct perspective that she adopts for the largest part of her narration is innovative whereas the vampiric point of view which she assumes in *Midnight Sun* is intertextual. Concepts of good and evil underline the revenant's potential to inhabit every angle of presentation ranging from intimate friend to uncomplicated evil. The vampire's position in society shows its prevailing status as an outsider, a characteristic that is also Byronic. Meyer's treatment of the star-crossed lovers theme (chapter 5.2.), regarding the obstacles the lovers have to face, is of great intertextual productivity as it offers many parallels to *Pride and Prejudice* as well as *Romeo and Juliet*. Supported by direct references and by means of interfigurality, Meyer's lovers also illustrate the fatality and irreversibility of their love as it is already displayed in *Romeo and Juliet* and *Wuthering Heights*, again relying on both works on a structural level. Meanwhile, Meyer's adoption of *Frankenstein* and *Rosemary's Baby*, although only implicitly linked to both works, proves intertextually potent in the fear of and for the monstrous vampire hybrid. Once more, in her depiction of the damsel in distress and the anti-mother as well as the incorporation of structural elements such as letters and articles Meyer orientates herself on already established motifs and pretextual sources such as Stoker's *Dracula* (chapter 5.3.).

2. Methodology

In order to examine structures, themes, and characters through the deployment of an intextextual method, it will be first of all necessary to decide which intertextual approach is most efficient for an analysis of the *Twilight* series. By the help of an intertextual analysis it will be possible to clearly determine the constituents in Meyer's work that refer to pretextual sources and in which degree these parts rely on earlier texts. However, it will also highlight which components are truly innovative in Meyer's series.

To accomplish this analysis it will be further beneficial to introduce and determine some of the most important narratological constituents of the *Twilight* saga such as the narrator and point of view as well as themes, motifs, and symbols in order to complement an intertextual analysis of the series.

2.1. INTERTEXTUALITY: A STRUCTURALIST APPROACH

By characterizing the interrelation between a text and its pretexts, these being the texts a given work draws on in order to extend and enforce its meaning, intertextuality is the study of how a text's meaning is shaped by help of other works. This idea was initially based on Michail Bachtin's theory of dialogism. It was then further expanded into a concept deducing that every text functions in an intertextual relation to other works and thus to a "texte général", a term coined by Julia Kristeva. She also developed the term "intertextuality" in the 1960s. Kristeva's poststructural approach that regards every text as an accumulation of an infinite number of preceding texts is, however, not adjuvant in carrying out an intertextual analysis of a literary text. Therefore, the deployed intertextual approach today is most of the time a structuralist one.[5] With a focus on pretexts whose integration in the given work is often intended by the author and can further also be noticed by the reader, an approach to intertextuality was developed[6] that could be used to analyze texts in relation to their pretexts, or, as Gérard Genette calls them, hypotexts. Contrary to the poststructural debate, the

---

[5] For further information on the two contrary approaches to intertextuality see Arne Klawitter and Michael Ostheimer, *Literaturtheorie – Ansätze und Anwendungen* (Göttingen: Vandenhoeck & Ruprecht, 2008) 93-105, Heinrich F. Plett, "Intertextualities," *Intertextuality*, ed. Heinrich F. Plett (Berlin; New York: Walter de Gruyter, 1991) 3-29, and Manfred Pfister, "Konzepte der Intertextualität," *Intertextualität: Formen, Funktionen, anglistische Fallstudien*, eds. Ulrich Broich and Manfred Pfister (Tübingen: Max Niemeyer Verlag, 1985) 1-30.
[6] In opposition to the poststructuralist approach which claims that every text is part of a universal text (Julia Kristeva), the structuralist hermeneutic approach takes up a different definition of the text and applies a descriptive concept of intertextuality. The approach is represented by literary critics such as Karlheinz Stierle and Gérard Genette who developed the first typology of intertextual references for literary texts.

8

structural hermeneutic approach is of a strongly descriptive nature and will, therefore, be applied in this study. Along with this approach goes the terminology of Ulrich Broich and Manfred Pfister's concept of intertextuality presented in their anthology *Intertextualität: Formen, Funktionen, anglistische Fallstudien.*

Elements of various pretexts can be transferred into a new text by means of quotation, allusion, parody, hints in the work's title and chapter titles as well as in other parts of the paratext and in the primary text. This disposition of elements is intended by the author and aims at broadening as well as specifying the text's relevance by means of pretextual elements. Meanwhile, un-intended transfer of elements through the author predominantly includes the use of stereotypes or character types and clichés. Therefore, the reader is the one who realizes the connections between text, interpretant – the effect that an intertextual reference has on the reader – and intertext[7] and can decode intertextual references[8].

Manfred Pfister develops six distinct criteria to analyze intertextual references in literary texts in his essay on the concepts of intertextuality. By the help of these criteria it is possible to judge the intensity of intertextual references within texts. Regarding the criterion of *referentiality*, intertextuality increases when the forerunning text broaches issues addressed in the given text and thereby approaches or distances itself from the pretext. Via the incorporation of marked intertextual references the author comments and interprets the pretext and thus depicts a new perspective on the text at hand. The term *communicativity* accounts for the degree of conscious intertextual reference on the side of the author as well as that of the recipient. Intertextuality is enhanced if references are clearly marked and if pretexts are known to the author as well as the reader. The criterion of *auto-reflexivity* signifies that the intertext itself, whose "constituents refer to constituents of one or several other texts [...] which creates structural relations between itself and other texts"[9], becomes a point of discussion within the successive text for the author. Intertextuality is then not only marked within the text but also becomes an issue in its own right and is judged and discussed due to its preconditions and its achievements. Pfister's concept of *structurality* deals with the overall integration of a pretext into a given text. As such, the intertextual intensity is the strongest if a pretext functions as a structural layer for the subsequent text and is additionally marked by

---

[7] Cf. Manfred Pfister, "Konzepte der Intertextualität," *Intertextualität: Formen, Funktionen, anglistische Fallstudien,* eds. Ulrich Broich and Manfred Pfister (Tübingen: Max Niemeyer Verlag, 1985) 20.
[8] Cf. Jörg Helbig, *Intertextualität und Markierung: Untersuchungen zur Systematik und Funktion der Signalisierung von Intertextualität* (Heidelberg: Universitätsverlag C. Winter, 1996) 72-75.
[9] Heinrich F. Plett, "Intertextualities," *Intertextuality,* ed. Heinrich F. Plett (Berlin; New York: Walter de Gruyter, 1991) 5.

frequent intertextual references such as quotations or allusions. The intertextual paradigm that evolves can be found throughout the whole text. Another criterion deals with the *selectivity* of intertextual elements and points out that pretextual references are selected on purpose and abstracted to fit into the new text. Accordingly, a quotation from the pretext that is inserted into the subsequent text functions as a *pars pro toto* in the new context. It stands for a particular concept or idea of the pretext. The last criterion, the concept of *dialogism*, refers back to Michail Bachtin's theory of dialogism and claims that a text "von umso höherer intertextueller Intensität ist, je stärker der ursprüngliche und der neue Zusammenhang in semantischer und ideologischer Spannung zueinander stehen"[10]. The intertextual reference is markedly strong if the intertext's new idea opposes its original meaning in the pretext or if it, in any form, satirizes the initial text by its context in the subsequent one.

However, Manfred Pfister's criteria are not exclusive and other aspects within the realm of intertextuality need to be considered, too. Intertextual references within a text can be marked or un-marked and, in addition, varying degrees of markedness exist ranging from literal to non-literal references. While a quotation through the use of inverted commas is a clearly marked intertextual device referring to a certain text, the allusion to a motif deployed anew can be rather obscure to the reader and sometimes even to the author. Meaningful words or phrases can evoke a complete set of distinct pretexts. The recognition of intertextual structures and references also depends on the reader's ability and knowledge of former texts that allow them to spot these signals. In looking at the literary text as one of the most prominent sources for intertextuality, it will be further necessary to consider intertextual markers that occur in the paratext, as well. These pretextual signs can appear in every aspect of the paratext, in prefaces and epilogues, titles and subtitles as well as in mottoes or footnotes. "Autoren [können] die intertextuellen Bezüge ihrer Werke natürlich auch in Äußerungen markieren, die nicht im Zusammenhang mit diesen Werken publiziert werden"[11]. Such statements pointing out further potential intertextual references can be found in interviews or other forms of commentary, such as letters or an author's list of favorite books, made public by the author.

Whether characters are aware of these intertextual references and act accordingly is also relevant. Characters might read other texts and discuss or even identify or distance themselves from the texts they read, which consequently creates more intertextual references.

---

[10] Pfister, "Konzepte der Intertextualität," 29.
[11] Ulrich Broich, "Formen der Markierung von Intertextualität," *Intertextualität: Formen, Funktionen, anglistische Fallstudien,* eds. Ulrich Broich and Manfred Pfister (Tübingen: Max Niemeyer Verlag, 1985) 38.

Wolfgang G. Müller calls such characters "reading protagonist[s]"[12] that empathize with literary figures and structure their own actions subsequently. Intertextuality is further intensified if pretexts appear within the text as physical objects such as books or if pretextual literary figures make their appearance within the new literary context. Additional markers can be set that are only recognizable by the readership but covert to the fictional heroes. Characters' names and fictional places can bear intertextual significance. Furthermore, changes in typeface and diction can mark intertextual references and can point to a certain pretext.

Another important aspect within the study of intertextuality is interfigurality which describes the "interrelations that exist between characters of different texts"[13]. Re-used names are "one of the most prominent meaning-generating devices in literary name-giving"[14] although they are also often used in altered forms through clipping or addition. However, not solely names are transported into new contexts but often also a character's physical appearance and character traits. Nevertheless, a complete identification with pretextual figures can only rarely be achieved due to the new literary context. Intertextual figures create "a characteristic tension between similarity and dissimilarity with their models from the pre-texts"[15], highlighting particular character traits while others are diminished. Intertextual characters dominantly appear if fictional heroes are modeled according to a heroic tradition or already established character types.

However, intertextual references can go even further than simply being markers of a numbered set of pretexts in a given text. References can also be made to a whole group of texts or a subgenre such as the Gothic novel in order to emphasize the appearance of elements in the subsequent text which the initial texts already share. In this case there is no specific pretext but rather a large number of texts that share common characteristics with the given text. The intertextual device in the new text can be found on every distinct discourse level of the text. Re-used figures also belong to this type of intertextuality if they derive from a heroic tradition or are considered as literary archetypes. The borderline between intertextual references that only have one singular source text and those that refer to a set of texts is rather intangible.

---

[12] Wolfgang G. Müller, "Interfigurality: A Study on the Interdependence of Literary Figures," *Intertextuality*, ed. Heinrich F. Plett (Berlin; New York: Walter de Gruyter, 1991) 116.
[13] Ibid., 101.
[14] Ibid., 103.
[15] Ibid., 109.

Given that the concept of intertextuality is an approach that is extensive and highly flexible, it can also be applied to non-literary texts. This kind of texts such as newspaper articles or letters can be included in an intended text as well as literary texts from differing genres. Thus, a poem that is inserted into a novel's paratext or recited within the novel's plot has intertextual significance and can broaden or clarify the given text's meaning. Moreover, an intertextual reference in a text permits the reader to draw conclusions about the pretext and its constituents. More than a simple repetition, the dialogue that is created between two texts enforces the intertext's meaning in the pretext or modernizes its proposition through modification and thus alters its significance. Another dimension of meaning is added in the new text which is furthermore enriched. Not exclusively bound to written works, intertextuality can transgress the realm of texts as well. Intermediality, "die Intertextualität zwischen Texten in verschiedenen Medien"[16], analyzes the processing of texts into movies, theater productions or pieces of music and vice versa. New forms of intertextual reference arise in which the potential intertextual relevance increases when the pretext is reduced so that the new text gains in importance.

However, authors who consciously highlight intertextual references to pretexts in order to emphasize particular passages of their work often utilize diverse markers of varied degrees of markedness simultaneously. References to one and the same source text can, thus, accumulate or abate throughout the given text.

Stephenie Meyer's *Twilight* series is interspersed with intertextual references in its themes, characters, and structure. Quotations from diverse literary texts are numerous and sometimes highlighted through its position in the paratext. Allusions to thematic intertextualities are also frequent though some themes such as the monster-creation-theme of *Frankenstein* or the motif of improbable conception in *Rosemary's Baby* are fundamental to the terminal part of the series but are not directly referred to throughout the novel. As a consequence of this other themes are more dominant in the narrative. In addition, intertextual clichés and character types – impersonated by Bella, Edward, Jacob, and Reneé, or Victoria – are manifest, as well, as will be shown in the course of this study.

All of the categories that Manfred Pfister elaborates on can be applied to the *Twilight* saga with varying degrees of intensity. *Twilight* approaches themes, motifs, and characters of its pretexts in a critical manner and re-interprets and re-evaluates aspects of the anteceding texts. This criterion is highly productive. Several references to pretexts are clearly marked

---

[16] Horst Zander, "Intertextualität und Medienwechsel," *Intertextualität: Formen, Funktionen, anglistische Fallstudien,* eds. Ulrich Broich and Manfred Pfister (Tübingen: Max Niemeyer Verlag, 1985) 178.

through quotations within the saga so that the author and the readers are aware of these links and the intertextual intensity is, thus, of great extent. Directly or indirectly, the intertext itself is frequently commented on by the author but only selectively discussed by characters within the series. However, it is frequently referred to if the intertextual reference is quoted and part of the narration and not only of the paratext. Then the characters within the narrated world know its meaning and source and usually comment on it which makes these references productive. Most of the time, these quotations or allusions are crucial to the pretext's composition and thus chosen according to the criterion of *selectivity*. The criterion of *structurality* is productive in varying degrees throughout all the parts of the tetralogy. Literary as well as media-based pretexts function as layers for every distinct novel and while in *Twilight* and *Breaking Dawn* these layers are rather obscure, they are marked by quotations and directly pointed to in *New Moon* and *Eclipse*. References are allocated throughout the whole text. Pfister's final criterion, the criterion of *dialogism*, is in parts productive if one thinks of the construction of the postmodern vampire and the references to Stoker's *Dracula* which are satirical.

Intertextual references, most of the time quotations from pretexts as well as allusions in chapter titles, can be found in the paratext and thus intensify *Twilight*'s overall intertextual significance. Pretextual literary figures that reappear in *Twilight* are not at all productive in the series. However, a limited number of characters are aware of distinct traits that they share with their figural ancestors and, therefore, add to the productivity of the criterion of *auto-reflexivity*. System references as to the Gothic novel, the literary vampire tradition or the Byronic hero are also frequent but they are only rarely marked by quotations and thus rather obscure. Inserted newspaper articles, letters and notes intensify the overall intertextual dialogue of the work.

Consequently, the *Twilight* saga and its themes, characters, and structure are intertextually productive in various ways and on distinct layers.

2.2. THE NARRATOLOGICAL APPROACH

The narratological approach that will be applied in order to achieve a coherent and thorough intertextual analysis of the *Twilight* series is primarily focused on the narrator and his point of view as well as the main themes, motifs, and symbols that interweave the saga. In

13

combination with a structuralist intertextual approach it will be possible to show similarities as well as disparities between the given texts and their pretexts.

2.2.1. Point of View and the Narrator

The narrator presents the portrayed world to the reader. He comments on actions that take place within the narrative framework, interprets the characters' motivations, influences the reader's empathy towards certain characters, and develops a system of social codes for the narrated world and the perception of it[17]. Franz K. Stanzel distinguishes between three different types of narrator: third-person narrator, first-person narrator, and figural narrator. He further differentiates between narrative mode (narrator and reflector), perspective (point of view, internal and external perspective), as well as person[18].

The first-person narrator that is also evident in Stephenie Meyer's *Twilight* series incorporates a large number of functions and offers various implications for the plot. Not every first-person narrator merges with the figure of the hero or heroine. Some first-person narrators tell their story from the periphery, thus commenting and judging other characters' actions, functioning as a witness and observer or acting "as memorialist for a collective experience"[19]. To fuse the narrator's identity with a fictional character often gives the narrative an atmosphere of authenticity and thus many implausible stories are told through the eyes of a first-person narrator[20]. However, the display of consciousness through a character's thoughts and assumptions is an even more important feature of first-person narration. "Die Ich-Erzählsituation verifiziert [...] ihre Subjektivität, ihre Realität als Bewußtseinsinhalt [sic] der Ich-Gestalt, oder vielmehr als eine letztlich unauflösliche Vermengung von objektiver, dinglicher Außen- und subjektiver, ideeller Innenwelt"[21]. Therefore, the focus lies on the internal perspective of the narrator. His personality, viewpoint, and attitudes are presented to the reader and the portrayed world turns into a retrospection of moments experienced anew.

---

[17] Cf. Monika Fludernik, *Einführung in die Erzähltheorie* (Darmstadt: Wissenschaftliche Buchgesellschaft, 2006) 37f.
[18] Cf. Franz K. Stanzel, *Theorie des Erzählens* (Göttingen: Vandenhoeck und Ruprecht, [8]2008) 30ff.
[19] Dorrit Cohn, *Transparent Minds: Narrative Modes for Presenting Consciousness in Fiction* (Princeton, NJ: Princeton University Press, 1978) 204.
[20] Franz K. Stanzel, therefore, names several examples, among them: Thomas More's *Utopia* and Jonathan Swift's *Gulliver's Travels*, in his study *Typische Formen des Romans* (Göttingen: Vandenhoeck und Ruprecht, [10]1993) 29.
[21] Franz K. Stanzel, *Typische Formen des Romans* (Göttingen: Vandenhoeck und Ruprecht, [10]1993) 30.

Furthermore, the first-person narrator is always in some respects unreliable. "Er kann auf Grund seines Standortes in der Welt der Charaktere und auf Grund seiner Ausstattung mit einer auch körperlich determinierten Eigenpersönlichkeit [...] nur eine persönlich-subjektive [...] Ansicht von den erzählten Vorgängen haben"[22]. Additionally, the I-narrator of a quasi-autobiographical tale is characterized through his corporeal existence within the narrative and feels an existential urge to tell his story. The distinction between narrating self and experiencing self is also crucial since the narrating self has often undergone a process of psychic change and now mediates the story from a more knowing standpoint. Consequently, the narrating self can often no longer completely identify itself with the experiencing self since it has gained some desistance from the experiencing self. However, the narrating self can still recount events by not "adding information, opinions, or judgments that were not his during his past experience"[23]. An equilibrium between the telling qualities of the narrating self and the showing qualities of the experiencing self, thus, results in the ideal narrative situation.

A first-person narrator views the world through an internal perspective. As such a character is focalized by the narrator and his feelings, attitudes and thoughts are presented to the reader. Correspondingly, distinct features of the narrated world attract the readers' interest while others do not. Stanzel further claims that "in die Opposition Innenperspektive – Außenperspektive [...] auch der Gegensatz zwischen Perspektivismus und Aperspektivismus [eingeht]"[24]. As such, a character's internal perspective in a narrative tends to display a spatial perception rather than a chronological one. This perception of space can either be perspective, predominantly featured in a narrator's showing of events, or non-perspective, if the narrator applies the technique of telling. "Bei einer aperspektivischen Raumdarstellung bleibt die Orientierung im Raum unbestimmt, sie wird daher von jedem Leser auf Grund seiner individuellen Vorstellungsneigungen vorgenommen werden"[25]. Furthermore, the use of an internal perspective entails a limited point of view because the knowledge of the narrator can only be limited and subjective if it is tied to a first-person narrator. Sympathy or antipathy towards other figures can easily be displayed and techniques like the interior monologue or free indirect discourse create a sense of immediacy in the narration.

The narrative mode describes the discrepancy between the mediacy of telling and the immediacy of showing, or scenic presentation of events, in a narration. It constitutes the

---

[22] Stanzel, *Theorie des Erzählens*, 122f.
[23] Cohn, *Transparent Minds: Narrative Modes for Presenting Consciousness in Fiction*, 155.
[24] Stanzel, *Theorie des Erzählens*, 151.
[25] Ibid., 164.

distinction between the use of a narrator or a reflector to narrate events. "Eine *Erzählerfigur* erzählt, berichtet, zeichnet auf, teilt mit, [...] eine *Reflektorfigur* reflektiert, [...] nimmt wahr, empfindet, registriert, aber immer stillschweigend, denn sie ‚erzählt' nie"[26]. The reflector's consciousness is directly presented to the reader. An illusion of immediacy is generated through the reflector. Just as the presentation of a narration can shift from narrating self to experiencing self and vice versa so can the use of narrator and reflector vary within a narration. Consequently, aspects and events that could be crucial to the plot can be absent due to the strongly focused perspective of the reflector.

Stephenie Meyer's *Twilight* tetralogy is narrated through the eyes of the novel's heroine Bella Swan and her friend Jacob Black. The spheres of existence of the narrators and fictional characters are identical so that the narrators are also characters in the fictional world. While the heroine in *Twilight* is at the heart of the action and inhabits the role of the protagonist, Jacob as a narrator stands at the periphery of the narrated world and functions as an I-as-witness. He gives the reader insights from the standpoint of a mere outsider and judges other characters' actions accordingly. Furthermore, Bella's and Jacob's thoughts, feelings and attitudes are displayed as is their unreliability since an inner perspective is applied to both narrators. The narrating self is mainly evident in the first chapters of each part of the saga, while the experiencing self dominates the remaining text. However, the narrating self is still present every time parts of the narrative are summarized. The narrating self has not distanced itself from the experiencing self and thus does not criticize or judge the experiencing self. As such, the narrative mode that Meyer mainly applies due to the experiencing self is the method of showing "d. h. Spiegelung der fiktionalen Wirklichkeit im Bewußtsein [sic] einer Romangestalt, wobei im Leser die Illusion der Unmittelbarkeit seiner Wahrnehmung der fiktionalen Welt entsteht"[27].

Although a first-person narrator with an internal perspective and a limited point of view which influences the reader's sympathies and antipathies for certain characters narrates *Twilight*, the plot is told in a chronological manner and only occasionally interspersed by analepses. Spatial descriptions are mainly perspective if they are reflected by the experiencing self so that the orientation within a room is determined by the narrator. A sense of immediacy is achieved through the display of Bella's and Jacob's thoughts and feelings via interior monologues and free indirect discourse. Both characters variably function as narrators and reflectors within the plot and events such as the killings in Seattle in *Eclipse* remain obscure

---

[26] Ibid., 194.
[27] Ibid., 71.

to Bella as the reflector. The intertextual intensity of *auto-reflexivity* is further enhanced because the reader has access to Bella's and Jacob's thoughts and feelings.

2.2.2. Themes, Motifs, Symbols

A theme is the main idea that an author expresses within a novel. It is often abstract and can usually be interpreted in a variety of ways due to the characters of the novel, the conflict and the time the novel depicts, or the social circumstances that are questioned in the work. Thus, it is made concrete through its presentation in actions, persons, and images in the novel. Many themes that are taken up today have already been treated by previous authors. "Tatsächlich greifen jedoch viele Schriftsteller [...] auf überlieferte komplexe Handlungsgefüge [...] zurück, die schon einen gewissen Bekanntheitsgrad besitzen und die deshalb bestimmte Publikumserwartungen auslösen"[28]. Thus, every theme also has an intertextual dimension which makes it possible to compare the treatment of a specific theme in an author's work with earlier implementations of the same theme. *Twilight*'s main theme can be described as the falling in love against all human and non-human odds. Additionally, significant themes that contribute to the main theme are miscommunication, obstacles to a relationship, the star-crossed lovers as well as fear of and for the other. It is, therefore, no surprise that "Werke, die solche traditionsschwangeren Stoffe aufgreifen, normalerweise ein gesteigertes Maß an intertextuellen Bezügen [aufweisen]"[29].

Motifs are closely linked to a novel's themes. They are often recurring within the framework of a literary text and are also highly intertextual since other authors have often already dealt with the same motifs in the past. "Motive zeigen Personen und Sachen nicht isoliert, sondern in einen Zusammenhang, d. h. eine Situation, gestellt"[30]. Motifs usually help to develop the text's major themes. The most significant motif, and also a leitmotif, in the *Twilight* series is the lover's meadow as a *locus amoenus* and contrary to it the clearing as a place for athletic challenge and fight as a *locus terribilis*. Both of them have a constant place in the saga and reoccur at several points throughout the texts' plot. The clearing motif is one of the most significant motifs in the *Twilight* series since many meaningful decisions are made at these places. Other motifs that play an important role within the series and are highly

---

[28] Jost Schneider, *Einführung in die Roman-Analyse* (Darmstadt: Wissenschaftliche Buchgesellschaft, 2003) 28.
[29] Ibid., 29.
[30] Elisabeth Frenzel, *Stoff-, Motiv- und Symbolforschung* (Stuttgart: J. B. Metzler Verlag, [4]1978) 29.

intertextual are the vampire motif, the motif of light and darkness as opposing as well as overlapping concepts, the motif of drugs and addiction due to love, the lovers' conflict due to ancestry, rivalry in love, the rebel, the demonic seductress or *femme fatale* and the *femme fragile* among others.

Symbols are objects, characters, places, or colors that represent abstract ideas. Thus, a symbol has more meaning attributed to it then is obvious at first glance. "Ein dichterisches Symbol muß [sic] konkretes Ding oder echte Person im Handlungsgefüge sein"[31]. While the symbol itself is always something concrete in the story, its meaning is usually abstract although it still relates to the object itself. "Es kann nicht mit dem ausgetauscht werden, was es symbolisiert, und nicht wie das X einer Gleichung durch seinen wirklichen Wert ersetzt werden. Denn es ist zugleich das, für das es steht [...] zugleich aber ist es mehr und anderes, unbestimmt und nicht identifizierbar"[32]. Thus, it stands for itself and also for something else evoking another level of meaning. Symbols that are important throughout the *Twilight* saga are people's scent, celestial bodies such as the distinct states of the moon, the stars, the meteor, and the sun, the hole in Bella's chest, or Edward's hallucinated voice among others.

---

[31] Ibid., 36.
[32] Ibid., 38.

18

3. Directions in Research

Naturally, there have always been a great number of commentaries and critical literary articles whenever a renowned piece of vampire fiction has been published throughout the last two centuries. A beginning was surely made with John Keats's poem *Lamia* (1820) and Samuel Taylor Coleridge's *Christabel* (1797). The vampire's first appearance in an English novel – John Polidori's *The Vampyre* (1819) based on a fragment composed by Lord Byron[33] – proved to be an immediate step into subsequent literature of that kind. As these were followed by the penny-dreadful *Varney the Vampire* (1847), Sheridan Le Fanu's *Carmilla* (1872) and Bram Stoker's *Dracula* (1897), the vampire became one of the most prominent motifs in nineteenth-century fantastic literature. Although a vast number of vampire novels and short stories were published in the subsequent seventy years[34] and beyond, critical works in the early decades of the twentieth century almost exclusively concentrated on the cultural varieties of vampirism in Europe. Fueled by the general rise of cultural studies but also due to the vampire's constant popularity on screen[35] and the success of Anne Rice's *The Vampire Chronicles* (1976-2003), literary criticism on vampire fiction has been vast since the 1970s. Especially *Dracula* and its psychological roots, in terms of homosexuality, incest, and female sexuality, as well as its relation to late nineteenth-century social and political issues were heavily debated. However, this discussion also allowed other works of vampire fiction to be considered for critical examination. Ever since the 1970s the literary vampire has been a favorite of scholarly attention and with *Dracula*'s centennial anniversary in 1997[36], its dominance in cinema and on TV[37] as well as the worldwide popularity of Stephenie Meyer's *Twilight* series this interest seems far from abating in the near future.

---

[33] Byron's fragmented story, later called "Fragment of a Novel", was obviously inspired by Goethe's ballad *Die Braut von Korinth*. Cf. Clemens Ruthner, *Am Rande: Kanon, Kulturökonomie und Intertextualität des Marginalen am Beispiel der (österreichischen) Phantastik im 20. Jahrhundert* (Tübingen: Francke, 2004) 140.

[34] For a detailed listing on the treatment of the vampire motif in English literature from 1900 until 1970 plus a list of twentieth-century movie adaptations see: Margaret L. Carter, "The Vampire," *Icons of Horror and the Supernatural: An Encyclopedia of Our Worst Nightmares, Volumes 1 and 2*, ed. S. T. Joshi (Westport, CT: Greenwood Press, 2007) 619-652.

[35] Already 12 major vampire films were produced until the mid-1970s, among them Hammer Studios' popular *Dracula* series with Christopher Lee and Roman Polanski's vampire satire *Dance of the Vampires* (1967).

[36] A newly revised Norton Critical Edition of Stoker's *Dracula*, edited by Nina Auerbach and David J. Skal, as well as the anthologies *Blood Read: The Vampire as Metaphor in Contemporary Culture*, edited by Joan Gordon and Veronica Hollinger, and *Bram Stoker's Dracula: Sucking through the Century 1897-1997*, edited by Carol Margaret Davison, were published among others.

[37] Among the most popular cinematic features are the *Blade* trilogy, the *Underworld* trilogy, and the sequel *Queen of the Damned* to the 1994 movie adaption of Anne Rice's *Interview with the Vampire*. Meanwhile, the television series *Buffy the Vampire Slayer* enjoyed great popularity on TV from 1997 until its seventh season finale in 2003.

3.1. VAMPIRES IN TWENTYFIRST-CENTURY LITERATURE

Margaret L. Carter spots the modern vampire in the 1970s when "vampire novels proliferated in unprecedented numbers"[38] and when the literary vampire was first portrayed as "domesticated" and re-humanized. In the last three decades, vampiric fiction and vampires have been sketched as the juxtaposition of supernatural and psychic vampirism, as the substitution of the demonically evil revenant by a more sympathetic vampire. This "new" type of vampire is a referential other with a free will in a secularized world. Authors begin to construct their vampiric novels based on a science fiction perspective or let their non-human heroes star in romances and thus create intimacy between the human and the undead other. Although already prominent since the 1990s, the vampire romance is still a productive subgenre of vampire fiction with the *Twilight* saga as one of its many descendants.

While scholarly work on Meyer's *Twilight* series has only begun to emerge within the last two years, literary criticism on postmodern vampire fiction has been around for more than a decade by now. Joan Gordon and Veronica Hollinger's anthology *Blood Read: The Vampire as Metaphor in Contemporary Culture* examines the transformations of the archetype from its nineteenth-century forebears. Gordon and Hollinger's work illuminates how the vampire reflects on changes in postmodern culture and becomes, just as Nina Auerbach claims in her study *Our Vampires, Ourselves*, the realism our culture finally understands and what every generation needs. Especially, Jules Zanger's "Metaphor into Metonymy: The Vampire next Door", Margaret L. Carter's "The Vampire as Alien in Contemporary Culture" and Veronica Hollinger's "Fantasies of Absence: The Postmodern Vampire" in *Blood Read* make predications on the "new" vampire of the twenty-first century and are, thus, relevant for this study. Certainly, these scholars are able to illustrate recent tendencies in vampire literature, such as the vampire on the boundary between intimate and referential other and the trend towards an absence of the fantastic other that leaves us "with the look into the mirror and [we] see nothing *but* ourselves"[39]. However, they do not comment on the latest developments in vampire fiction that series like Meyer's *Twilight* saga brought about by incorporating representations of fantastic otherness. Meyer's tetralogy displays the self and the other at the same time and extends notions of absence into a concept of denial for the vampiric bite and, consequently, the suspensive delay of sexual intimacy.

---

[38] Carter, "The Vampire," *Icons of Horror and the Supernatural*, ed. S. T. Joshi, 628.
[39] Veronica Hollinger, "Fantasies of Absence: The Postmodern Vampire," *Blood Read: The Vampire as Metaphor in Contemporary Culture*, eds. Joan Gordon and Veronica Hollinger (Philadelphia: University of Pennsylvania Press, 1997) 201.

Mary Y. Hallab's *Vampire God: The Allure of Undead in Western Culture* goes in a similar direction as Gordon and Hollinger do in their *Blood Read* anthology. Hallab intensively debates on the reliability of vampire literature in reflecting about the meaning of death and the human soul – a point of discussion that Meyer takes up in her series, as well. Margaret L. Carter's "Revampings of Dracula in Contemporary Fiction" as well as William Hughes' essay on "Fictional Vampires in the Nineteenth and Twentieth Centuries" name the distinct characteristics of the twenty-first century vampire. They precisely allude to the change of perspective, the re-humanization of the undead and the forms of abstinence such as the denial of the vampiric bite and the refusal of sexual closeness in postmodern vampire literature. Despite these works, none discusses *Twilight* as a potential commentary on postmodern culture in the context of a new culmination of vampire literature that is situated within the scope of an intertextual analysis, although Hallab's publication only dates back a year ago, to 2009.

3.2. LITERARY CRITICISM ON THE *TWILIGHT* SERIES

There are hardly any notable book-length publications in the scholarly field on Meyer's work so far. However, with the constantly growing popularity of the series and the associated vampire fiction genre an increasing number of scholarly work can be assumed to be published in the near future. Situating the novels within the framework of philosophical theory, Rebecca Housel and J. Jeremy Wisnewski's *Twilight and Philosophy: Vampires, Vegetarians and the Pursuit of Immortality* is one of the few critical works published so far, almost doing pioneer work on the subject. Within this anthology on morality, food analogies and the ethics of vegetarianism, as well as the question of divinity, Abigail E. Myers's paper "Edward Cullen and Bella Swan: Byronic and Feminist Heroes … or Not", draws special attention on the protagonists' disposition within heroic traditions. As a topic that has already been prominent among other scholars dealing with Byronic vampires in general but also with Meyer's vampires in particular, the question of Byronic heroism was also raised by Stephanie Mendoza's essay "From Dawn to Twilight: The Byronic Hero" and Teresa Cotsirilos's commentary "Bella and Byron: Stephenie Meyer's Twilight Series". Mendoza and Cotsirilos are able to shed a new and extremely interesting light on Edward Cullen's position within the heroic tradition of the Byronic hero. However, they are not fully sufficient since an intertextual scope, which can be considered fruitful for Meyer's work, is not applied to their considerations. Kate Cochran applies a basic intertextual focus in her scientific paper on "'An Old-fashioned Gentleman'? Edward's Imaginary History" as she situates the hero of Meyer's series in a line with a number of nineteenth-century Romantic heroes such as Darcy, Rochester, and Heathcliff. Notwithstanding Cochran's correct classification of Edward as an intertextual figure, she does not accomplish a thorough analysis of the hero's Byronic qualities but merely refers to overt intertextual references in the *Twilight* saga. The anthology *Twilight & History*[40] that also contains Cochran's paper compiles a vivid analysis of the series' most important characters classifying them in terms of their own fictional history but then again does not consider them along intertextual parameters.

Other scholars such as Gabriella Calchi Novati and Kirsten Stevens are concerned with otherness, selfhood and the family in *Twilight*[41]. Meyer's personal religious views and their effect on *Twilight* are also frequently being debated on. Leonie Viola Thöne points out the various cornerstones of Mormonism in her work *Die Figur Edward Cullen: Moderner Mormonen-Missionar oder Vampir-Romantiker?*[42] and puts them in connection to the series and the moral values it conveys. A similar approach is taken in Marc E. Shaw's essay "For the Strength of Bella? Meyer, Vampires, and Mormonism" published in the *Twilight and Philosophy* anthology. However, neither Thöne nor Shaw adopts an intertextual scope to their analyses.

One of the first comparative analysis was done by Elizabeth Nelson in her essay "Monstrous Desire: Love, Death, and Marriage from Eros and Psyche to Edward and Bella" by reporting on the similarities in the tale of *Cupid and Psyche* and *Twilight*. Although highly interesting, Nelson's essay does not approach textually-evident intertextual references in the vampire saga. She more or less draws her conclusions from content-related analogies and an examination of the unequal, but unique relationship of the two couples.

So far the only intertextual analysis based on textually-evident material as well as covert intertextual markers from the *Twilight* saga is carried out by Glennis Byron in her paper "'As one dead': *Romeo and Juliet* in the 'Twilight' zone". In her essay Byron discusses

---

[40] Cf. Nancy R. Reagin, ed., *Twilight & History* (New Jersey: John Wiley & Sons, Inc., 2010).
[41] Cf. Gabriella Calchi Novati, "Who we might be – Performing the Potentialities of Otherness and Selfhood: Stephenie Meyer's Twilight Saga," *Inter-Disciplinary.Net: A Global Network for Dynamic Research and Publishing*, 2009, 1 Nov. 2010 < http://www.inter-disciplinary.net/wp-content/uploads/2009/08/g-calchi-novati-m7-draft-paper.pdf> and Kirsten Stevens, "Meet the Cullens: Family, Romance and Female Agency in 'Buffy the Vampire Slayer' and 'Twilight'," *Slayage – The Journal of the Whedon Studies Association*, 8.1 [29] 64 pars., 1 Nov. 2010 <http://slayageonline.com/essays/slayage29/Stevens.htm>.
[42] Cf. Leonie Viola Thöne, *Die Figur Edward Cullen: Moderner Mormonen-Missionar oder Vampir-Romantiker?* (Dresden: edition Wissenschaft, 2009).

22

the parallels of Meyer's second novel, *New Moon*, and *Romeo and Juliet*. She claims that in modern-day adaptations of Shakespeare's tragedy the conflict between the lovers and their families is the focal point of action as "drastic measures are quite unnecessary. The focus is instead on conflict, on the 'ancient grudge' (Prologue: 3) and [...] on the autonomy of desire"[43]. Moreover, she makes the assumption that the spontaneous love which is celebrated in Shakespeare's play is rather threatening and dangerous to the characters' authentic identity in Meyer's series. However, although Byron develops an interesting comparative analysis of both texts regarding their differing conceptions of love, her essay does not touch on any other intertextual relations of the saga. She also does not consider the characters' further potential for interfigurality and does not adopt a straightforward concept of intertextuality.

---

[43] Glennis Byron, "'As one dead': Romeo and Juliet in the 'Twilight' zone," *Gothic Shakespeares*, eds. John Drakakis and Dale Townshend (Abingdon; New York: Routledge, 2008) 170.

4. Man of Feeling, Byronic Hero and the Nineteenth-Century Vampire

The literature of the eighteenth and nineteenth century in England spawned a vast literary heroic tradition. With the emergence of the hero type of the Man of Feeling that the enormous production of sentimental literature brought about in the eighteen century a hero was created who was feeling, sensible and not adapted to the cruelties that life posed to him. Despite his fragility the Man of Feeling had a significant impact on the nineteenth-century heroic tradition. The Byronic hero, probably the literary hero with the largest number of contemporary and popular descendants up until the present day, also adopted some of his qualities from this sensitive eighteenth-century hero.

As the Byronic hero's constitution is based on a wide range of hero types that were prominent throughout the preceding decades of his evolution, his ability to represent multi-faceted characters endows him with the capability to challenge prevailing limitations and exceed them. This is a characteristic which he also imparted on the nineteenth-century vampire who was partially designed after him. Throughout Romanticism and beyond the vampire served as the most favored example of the fantastic other as it transgressed boundaries and presented various possibilities to exemplify evil through its manifold faces.

In this chapter it is, thus, essential to take a closer look at the peculiar hero types in English literature, as already mentioned, and the influence they have on the formation of the vampire in nineteenth-century literature. As such, a new light is shed on Meyer's construction of her vampires and heroes.

4.1. THE MAN OF FEELING

The sentimental literature in eighteenth-century England gave rise to a new hero type that was to influence its heroic descendants in the years that followed. Sensibility "came to denote the faculty of feeling, the capacity for extremely refined emotion and a quickness to display compassion for suffering"[44]. The movement was expedited through prayers for natural benevolence in the churches of that time[45] and the philosophical works of the third Earl of Shaftesbury, who is nowadays often referred to as "the 'father' of eighteenth-century

---

[44] Janet Todd, *Sensibility: An Introduction* (London; New York: Methuen, 1986) 7.
[45] Especially the latitudinarian Anglican churches emphasized the significance of benevolence.

sentimentalism"[46]. Sentimental impulses in literature are, however, recurrent and were already imminent in medieval morality plays and Elizabethan and Jacobean drama, whereas the centrality of sentiment and pathos is fairly new in eighteenth-century literature and moral philosophy. With its aim to conduct its readers and to manipulate them as to provoke tears, sentimental currents in literature drew on archetypical victims such as chaste, suffering women and sensitive, benevolent men to convey feelings to its readership. "A sentimental work moralizes more than it analyses and emphasis is not on the subtleties of a particular emotional state but on the communication of common feeling from sufferer or watcher to reader or audience"[47].

This also affected the text's appearance. Prescribed words such as 'virtue' and 'esteem' became conventional, repetitive and often overcharged through intensifying prefixes. The sentence structure was interrupted by dashes, asterisks or brackets to feign the reactive and unstable flow of sensibility. Furthermore, "terms and structures are repeated to heighten intensity"[48]. The overall text is presented as fragmented as "absence is one of the major tropes of sentimental fiction"[49]. Therefore, gaps are inserted as pretense of missing chapters to underline the distinct qualities of extreme feeling and the inarticulateness of sensibility. However, this also offers the narrator the possibility to narrate episodes of distress without the burden of dull connections. Sentimental elements further had an influence on Gothic fiction as well as Romantic poetry[50] after the 1770s.

The Man of Feeling, the hero type that was created in sentimental literature, is a vulnerable, sensitive man. Named after Henry Mackenzie's novel of sentimentality *The Man of Feeling* which was published in 1771 at the peak of literary sensibility, the hero's "benevolence arose from fellow feeling and ready identification with the unfortunate"[51]. The Man of Feeling proved not only to be important in the eighteenth century but had a significant impact on the conception of the Romantic Byronic hero of the nineteenth century. Mackenzie's novel of sensibility became one of the most popular of the day[52] and its author was initially highly appraised for his work.

---

[46] Peter L. Thorslev Jr., *The Byronic Hero: Types and Prototypes* (Minneapolis: University of Minnesota, 1962) 36.
[47] Todd, *Sensibility*, 4.
[48] Ibid., 5.
[49] Henry Mackenzie, *The Man of Feeling*, ed. Brian Vickers (Oxford: Oxford University Press, 2009) xvi.
[50] Cf. Todd, *Sensibility*, 9.
[51] Michael Bell, *Sentimentalism, Ethics and the Culture of Feeling* (New York: Palgrave, 2000) 181.
[52] Cf. Michael Gassenmeier, *Der Typus des 'Man of Feeling': Studien zum sentimentalen Roman des 18. Jahrhunderts in England* (Tübingen: Max Niemeyer Verlag, 1972) 124.

The character of a Man of Feeling, who often belongs to the middle class or lower gentry, is above all defined by his amiable qualities. He believes in the innocence of heart, is excessively compassionate in his actions, and appears extraordinary in his readiness to help others. Therefore, he "presupposes the doctrines of the essential goodness of human nature"[53]. The combination of these character traits causes the rise in prominence of the Man of Feeling in the middle of the eighteenth century. He often has a pale complexion, is inclined to illnesses and fever due to his fragile constitution and sometimes even seems effeminate. Through his simplicity of manners, careless generosity, and sweet sensibility he stands in strong contrast to the uncaring, decadent and often unjust world he inhabits. Too exquisite for vulgarity and for the selfishness of the world "the man of feeling [...] avoided manly power and assumed the womanly qualities of tenderness and susceptibility"[54]. Thus, he frequently looses the balance between sense and sensibility through his excess of sensitivity and his naivety[55].

However, the victims whom he helps in their desperation, the suffering women, the powerless servants, and the exquisite men, are mere props to display the hero's virtues and amiable qualities. Their pain and grief is overplayed through the Man of Feeling's virtues which "on the whole occur defensively and impotently and their possession always creates the victim"[56]. His acts of sensibility are mere ineffectualities as they bring the victim into being in the first instance. They are existent in order to present and exhibit the hero's sentimental characteristics and his benevolence to emotional display in helping them ease their pain and suffering. Besides, sentimental novels have a strong instructional character because "incidents occur solely for the maxims they produce, and there is no interest in the personalities necessary to create such incidents"[57]. The hero's virtue first and foremost creates the necessity of victims to accentuate his own virtue.

Mackenzie's vulnerable hero of sensibility, Harley, shows the mechanisms of a hostile and cruel world on a thoroughly sentimental man. His journey to a capitalist London presents the city as a mere place of animosity to which, in contrast, the countryside appears to be a haven of open-heartedness and benevolence – a dichotomy between urban and rural settings that Meyer similarly picks up in her *Twilight* series. The people who cross his way in town are either suffering victims to whom London has proved to be a fatal decision or they are

---

[53] Thorslev, *The Byronic Hero*, 21.
[54] Todd, *Sensibility*, 88f.
[55] Cf. Gassenmeier, *Der Typus des 'Man of Feeling'*, 129.
[56] Todd, *Sensibility*, 94.
[57] Ibid., 91.

scoundrels in their behavior and attitudes and the source of misery to others. The city highlights the uncorrupted nature und innocence of the male hero but also strangely emphasizes his separation and alienation from society. The curate who hands over Harley's papers to the narrator tells him that he saw Harley "playing at te-totum with the children, on the great stone at the door of our grave-yard"[58]. The hero, with children as his only friends, stands alone in an uncivil world that is free of kindness, further underlined through the distance between narrator, fictional editor and sentimental hero. However, his solidarity is a form of self-imposed isolation, thus heightening his distance from other human beings.

As one of the major eighteenth-century hero types[59] the Man of Feeling is "set apart from common men because of his peculiar and exacerbated sensitivity, although he shares the professed moral and social codes of his neighbors"[60]. He accepts the rules of the community he lives in although he is a mere outsider to that society. With his whimsical constitution, timid temperament – almost to the point of cowardice – and natural goodness the Man of Feeling is, therefore, far from becoming a rebel in his time. Although the Man of Feeling lends some of his own, most dominant characteristics to the Romantic hero type of the Byronic hero and has a "great survival power in the literature of the times and of the succeeding age"[61], he dies in the end of a mere excess of sensibility proving his inaptness of dealing with his surroundings once more. His chosen isolation is the "very antithesis of the moralistic Man of Feeling's emphasis on social sympathy"[62]. It explains the succeeding self-imposed isolation of later Romantic hero types to which the Man of Feeling has been a crucial predecessor.

4.2. THE BYRONIC HERO

The Romantic hero with the most significant consequences for European literature in the nineteenth century was by far the Byronic hero. As an incorporation of different eighteenth- and nineteenth-century hero types the Byronic hero emerges as the epitome of the Romantic hero. Certainly, with such prominent impersonators as Emily Brontë's Heathcliff and

---

[58] Mackenzie, *The Man of Feeling*, ed. Brian Vickers, 4.
[59] The other important hero type of the eighteenth century is the Child of Nature according to Peter L. Thorslev Jr.'s study on eighteenth- and nineteenth-century hero types and the Byronic Hero in Peter L. Thorslev Jr., *The Byronic Hero: Types and Prototypes* (Minneapolis: University of Minnesota, 1962).
[60] Thorslev, *The Byronic Hero*, 21.
[61] Ibid., 35.
[62] Ibid., 39.

Charlotte Brontë's Edward Rochester as well as their contemporary successors the continuous attraction of this hero remains untainted until the present day[63]. However, apart from these appealing heroes the repetitive confusion of the hero type with the character of its name giver, Lord Byron, has added to the popularity envisioning a true flesh and blood Byronic hero. Nevertheless, the Byronic hero has always been a combination of various elements taken from distinct preceding hero types, sometimes combined and sometimes not which led to a great variety of descendants.

4.2.1 Types and Prototypes

Over the decades the Byronic hero embraced the Man of Feeling's intensity of emotion without adopting his whimsicalness and fragile stature. This great exposure of emotional behavior let to a more sympathetic demeanor of the nineteenth-century hero. It was further only a small step from the self-imposed isolation of the eighteenth-century hero type to the poetic individualism which is immensely characteristic for the Romantic hero. The Gothic villain of the eighteenth century also influenced the conception of the Byronic hero and had a huge influence on the creation of Byron's hero, Manfred. With his inherent mystery, ingenious mind and irrepressible will and evil the Gothic villain is of immense psychological complexity and rebels against society although he "acknowledges the moral codes [...] and his own wickedness in violating those codes"[64]. His origins are often unknown or somehow mysterious although most of the time he is of an aristocratic upbringing. As such "an air of mystery is his dominant trait, and characteristic of all his acts. Frequently it is increased by an aura of past secret sins"[65], which distinguishes the Gothic villain from other hero types of his time.

Physically, the Gothic villain is strikingly handsome, of a pale complexion, has dark hair and is tall. However, most noticeable are his eyes – a feature which was also taken over by the Byronic hero besides the "defiant energy of a Gothic villain"[66] which he inherited, too.

---

[63] Cf. Atara Stein, *The Byronic Hero in Film, Fiction, and Television* (Carbondale: Southern Illinois University Press, 2004) and Atara Stein, "Immortals and Vampires and Ghosts, Oh My!: Byronic Heroes in Popular Culture," *Romanticism and Contemporary Culture* 2002 Romantic Circles, 1 Nov. 2010 <http://www.rc.umd.edu/praxis/contemporary/stein/stein.html>.
[64] Thorslev, *The Byronic Hero*, 53.
[65] Ibid., 54.
[66] Fred Botting, *Gothic* (London; New York: Routledge, 2003) 98.

Furthermore, he is the one "from which the prototypical literary vampire would descend"[67] with Dracula as its epitome. His misogynist delight in persecuting women takes every possible redeeming quality from him. In any case, the merge of the Gothic villain with the Hero of Sensibility that predominantly took place in the Gothic drama at that time turned out to "mitigate all of his other crimes, no matter how Gothic"[68]. Therefore, the Gothic villain becomes a remorseful hero and "his remorse is ever more emphasized at the expense of his villainy"[69], secluding the transformation from villain to hero.

The Noble Outlaw as one of the major hero types of Romanticism emblematizes, just as all the Romantic heroes, isolation due to birth, nature, breeding, or moral choices as well as rebellion against society. Romantic heroes are "fundamentally and heroically rebellious, at first against society only, and later against the natural universe or against God himself"[70]. This tendency towards radical individualism is purely Romantic. In combination with the insatiable thirst for knowledge and the drift to *hubris* it leads to one of the most prominent depictions of the Byronic hero in *Manfred* in which the protagonist is "egozentrisch und leidenschaftlich, vereinsamt in seiner Größe, schuldgequält und lebensmüde"[71]. The Noble Outlaw also lent his courtesy towards women to the Byronic hero. As such, the Noble Outlaw, and later on the Byronic hero, is displayed as a largely sympathetic character and never cruel or sadistic by nature though being "wronged either by intimate personal friends, or by society in general"[72].

The Byronic hero inherited his eternal "thirst for absolute knowledge and his lust for experience"[73] from the Faustian hero rooted in Germany. Thorslev claims that Faust belongs to the line of Heroes of Sensibility who later resulted in the Byronic hero. One of the most important characteristics of these heroes, thus, is their *Weltschmerz*; a "longing for some intellectual and moral certainty" opposed by the desire "toward a positive and passionate assertion of oneself as an individual"[74] constituting a remarkable character trait of the Byronic hero. However, the superhuman qualities that the Byronic hero most certainly asserts in his rebellion against God and society are traits which he assumed from such characters as Cain or the wandering Jew. This rebellion reached its climax in the character of the Romantic

---

[67] Kathryn McGinley, "Development of the Byronic Vampire: Byron, Stoker, Rice," *The Gothic World of Anne Rice*, eds. Gary Hoppenstand and Ray B. Browne (Bowling Green, OH: Bowling Green State University Popular Press, 1996) 73.
[68] Thorslev, *The Byronic Hero*, 55.
[69] Ibid., 61.
[70] Ibid., 66.
[71] Gerhart Hoffmeister, *Byron und der europäische Byronismus* (Darmstadt: Wissenschaftliche Buchgesellschaft, 1983) 25.
[72] Thorslev, *The Byronic Hero*, 69.
[73] Ibid., 87.
[74] Ibid., 89.

Prometheus fighting for individual liberty and bringing the sentiment of suffering out of love to a new height "in an alien and amoral universe"[75]. Therefore, the inferential isolation and individualism that the Byronic hero feels result in the creation of his own human values and "the 'sins' of which he repents are transgressions of his own peculiar moral codes"[76]. Society's moral codes do not apply as the Byronic hero creates his own rules. Nevertheless, not only does Cain possess superhuman characteristics. Due to his crime he is also doomed to immortality and eternal wandering just as Coleridge's mariner in *The Rime of the Ancient Mariner* – a characteristic that was also assigned to the Byronic hero as neither Manfred nor Brontë's Heathcliff are allowed to end their lives of their own free will. Furthermore, Cain has an inherent death wish linked to his strong feeling of *Weltschmerz* since he cannot achieve death in an ordinary way.

The modern-day Byronic hero still bears all the qualities that the eighteenth and nineteenth century endowed him with. He is still the dark, brooding rebel and skeptic with a great capability for remorse and an inherent mysterious aura. Just as his predecessors "he cannot be reintegrated into society, even if he has benefited that society with his heroic actions. He must be rehumanized, exiled, and/or destroyed"[77]. Alien to his readership he remains the arrogant outcast who cannot relate to others but in his self-autonomy and power bears a strong appeal for his audience. Whenever a Byronic hero is finally rehumanized, "he leaves the audience content with their own condition and the ability to identify with the hero"[78], thus making him sympathetic. Stein further claims that contemporary successors of the Byronic hero are great, powerful leaders or protectors who envy others' humanity because it is the one thing that they cannot achieve themselves by their own power. They are even "much more likely to take on a *successful* leadership role in the battle against oppression"[79]. Contemporary heroes who stand in the tradition of Byronism like Batman, Eric Draven from the *The Crow* comics and movies or Anne Rice's Lestat from *The Vampire Chronicles* have no respect for institutionalized authorities. They take the law in their own hands and they are often "simultaneously judge, jury, and executioner to the villains, while imposing the equivalent of martial law on everybody else until justice is served"[80].

---

[75] Ibid., 121.
[76] Ibid., 152.
[77] Atara Stein, "Immortals and Vampires and Ghosts, Oh My!: Byronic Heroes in Popular Culture," <http://www.rc.umd.edu/praxis/ contemporary/stein/stein.html> 3rd paragraph.
[78] Atara Stein, *The Byronic Hero in Film, Fiction, and Television*, 3.
[79] Ibid., 10.
[80] Ibid., 31.

As such it is no surprise that Byronic qualities are also already inherent in the vampires of nineteenth-century literature. In their position as undeads they are peculiarly outsiders to society, always standing on the brink of the human community. Just as the vast number of Byronic heroes, they transgress boundaries due to their particular state of existence and their defiance of authority and institutionalized power. Kathryn McGinley, who puts vampires from Byron to Rice's works into a line of Byronic vampires, notes that "the Byronic hero already had many of the mythic qualities of the vampire"[81] because he displayed power, authority as well as beauty. The most admired and appealing Byronic attributes for self-destruction and self-reflection, however, are only hardly apparent in the vampires of the nineteenth century. Nevertheless, they become core characteristics of the modern vampire who lives in a secularized world.

4.3. THE NINETEENTH-CENTURY VAMPIRE AND ITS METAPHOR

From the intimate and overtly friendly vampiress to the power-seeking, well-groomed and apparently evil Count Dracula the reader is offered a number of diverse examples of literary nineteenth-century vampires. As the representation of the vampire differs, so does the metaphor it conveys leaving its symbolization as something peculiar evil the only constant in that time.

A closer look at the female vampire with its mythological origin in the Greek lamia and its nineteenth-century impersonators will be beneficial to decode the conception of sexuality and intimacy it transports. Meanwhile, the male vampire's presentation of power and alienation within Victorian society sheds a new light on that society and their superficialities that the vampire efficiently penetrates.

4.3.1. Lamia, the female Vampire, and Sexuality

The female vampire as presented in Keats's *Lamia*, Coleridge's *Christabel,* Sheridan Le Fanu's vampire tale *Carmilla* as well as Stoker's three abject vampire women and Lucy Westenra in *Dracula* descended from the Greek mythological figure of the lamia, a child-devouring creature who was punished by Hera for having an affair with Zeus. She, consequently, became a female demon with a serpent's tail, who feeds on her own offspring,

---

[81] McGinley, "Development of the Byronic Vampire," 73.

and served as the prototype for the literary vampire, a woman who seduces men to drink their blood and attain their love. In this form the vampire is depicted in Goethe's *Die Braut von Korinth* and Keats' *Lamia* to which "the prevailing image of the female vampire can be traced back to"[82]. Goethe's bride is a beautiful girl who is "wie der Schnee so weiß / Aber kalt wie Eis" (110-111) in her complexion. The young man's beloved is clearly dead:

> Seine Liebeswut
> Wärmt ihr starres Blut,
> Doch es schlägt kein Herz in ihrer Brust. (124-126)

Nevertheless, he adores her. As such, it is precisely his imposition on her that leads to the final disclosure. When her mother enters in the morning she catches the lovers red-handed and the girl admits that what she truly wants is "den schon verlornen Mann zu lieben, / Und zu saugen seines Herzens Blut" (178-179). The ballad highlights the varied conceptions "einer über den Tod hinausreichenden Liebschaft ins Romantische wie ins Fatale"[83].

Keats' *Lamia* also loves a young man, Lycius of Corinth. She is "some demon's mistress, or the demon's self" (56) restored from the shape of a serpent to her human form by Hermes. The "full-born beauty" (172) seduces Lycius and they are rejoicing themselves in their private sphere until he persuades her to marry him. When the sage Apollonius, the prototype for the later Van Helsing and Le Fanu's Dr. Hesselius, reveals Lamia's identity she retransforms into a serpent, "breath'd death breath" (299) and Lycius dies of a broken heart. Similar to Le Fanu's *Carmilla*, in Coleridge's *Christabel* the vampiric woman Geraldine seduces a young woman. Just like Lamia, Geraldine is exceedingly beautiful with her "silken robe of white / [...] gems entangled in her hair" (59-65). Determined by her vampiric nature she cannot pass "the threshold of the gate" (132) and the guard dog shows his distrust to her with "an angry moan" (148). *Christabel* exhibits the very first limitations that are put on vampires through folkloric and Christian belief as they were taken up in the twentieth-century movie adaptations of the motif. Le Fanu's Carmilla also preys on a young woman, Laura, who lives isolated with her father. Like preceding female vampires Carmilla although "portrayed with some sympathy"[84] not only drinks her beloved one's blood but also adores her human companion. She offers true and profound friendship to Laura who lives bereft of any female friends with her father and nurse in a castle in Styria.

What the nineteenth-century female vampire displays is a capacity to achieve true intimacy with a beloved one through the creation of a relationship that is characterized as a

---

[82] Carter, "The Vampire," *Icons of Horror and the Supernatural*, ed. S. T. Joshi, 622.
[83] Ruthner, *Am Rande*, 141.
[84] Carter, "The Vampire," *Icons of Horror and the Supernatural*, ed. S. T. Joshi, 627.

one-to-one binding. In this respect the female vampire differs greatly from its male counterpart who usually feeds on other women without the restrictions of a monogamic bonding. Creatures like Carmilla and Lamia show veritable companionship that exceeds the bonds of simple friendship. They not only arouse desire but actually enact it. The "female vampire is licensed to realize the erotic, interpenetrative friendship male vampires aroused and denied"[85]. They are depicted as alluring and seductive and in their enticement they are often terrifying as much as they are erotic as they accomplish forms of sexual intercourse with their beloved one. Wisker comments on the fact that they are "abject creatures whose voracious sexuality is a product of male transfer of what is both desired and feared"[86]. With their boundary-transgressing sexuality they violate societal norms and moral codes. Accordingly, they must be destroyed in the end, as Carmilla is by Dr. Hesselius, Lamia through the revelations of Apollonius or Dracula's three brides by the hand of Van Helsing to equilibrate the system of social norms.

However, they are not only mere lovers or intimate companions. Often they are also fatal to the ones they get close to. Lamia's retransformation into a serpent leads to Lycius' death out of grief while Laura gets almost completely drained out by Carmilla during their acquaintance. Both of them have disastrous effects on their companions and also Stoker's Lucy attempts to prey on her still human fiancé. All these ill-fated women are to some degree *femmes fatales*[87] in that they also threaten what they entice and they finally destroy whom they desire – "it is this double-edged appeal that makes [them] ... fatal in the first place"[88]. Although they still combine the characteristics of voluptuous seductress and uncorrupted virgin, they break the boundaries of familial roles and as in *Carmilla* and *Christabel* inhabit and antagonize the role of the mother. They present the terrors of maternal power as they are already inverted in the figure of the lamia devouring children instead of feeding them.

Stoker's female vampires are almost entirely reduced to their function as lamiae. *Dracula*'s three vampiresses as well as Lucy Westenra are restricted to prey on children by their male counterparts; either Dracula or Van Helsing interferes whenever they aim for a man. They are confined by their own beauty and voluptuousness as they arouse "a languorous

---

[85] Nina Auerbach, *Our Vampires Ourselves* (Chicago: University of Chicago Press, 1995) 39.
[86] Gina Wisker, "Love Bites: Contemporary Women's Vampire Fictions," *A Companion to the Gothic*, ed. David Punter (Malden, Mass.: Blackwell Publishers Ltd., 2000) 170.
[87] Cf. Eva Volkmer-Burwitz, *Tod und Transzendenz in der deutschen, englischen und amerikanischen Lyrik der Romantik und Spätromantik* (Frankfurt am Main: Peter Lang Verlag, 1987) 181-198.
[88] Silke Binias. *Symbol and Symptom: the Femme Fatale in English poetry of the 19th century and feminist criticism* (Heidelberg: Winter Universitätsverlag, 2007) 39.

ecstacy"[89] in their victim. As such, they are led thoroughly by their sensual desires, thus juxtaposing the mere innocence and purity of Mina Harker whom the diverse group of men attempts to protect. Female vampires come to represent a "repressed libido freed from restraint through an act analogous to sexuality"[90] that symbolizes emancipatory tendencies and the transgression of sexual boundaries. Their kisses function as "a euphemism for deeper intimacy"[91]. However, it is precisely this ambivalent mixture of sexual pleasure and fright that provokes terror and leads to the inevitable destruction of the female vampire to restore the antecedent order.

4.3.2. Power and Alienation, the Aristocratic male Vampire

The image of the male vampire of the nineteenth century was predominantly shaped through the hands of Polidori and Stoker along with the penny-dreadful *Varney the Vampire* whose authorship cannot be solved without a doubt until the present day[92]. Inspired by a fragmentary tale composed by Lord Byron, "modern genre of vampire fiction may be seen as perhaps the most vital and enduring of all the varied expressions of Byronism"[93], drawing on the person of Byron as well as his work[94].

Polidori's Lord Ruthven is an aristocratic vampire, a nobleman, who is remarkably attractive so that "female hunters after notoriety attempted to win his attention"[95]. As he goes on a journey to Greece with his companion, Aubrey, and is wounded by robbers he binds Aubrey to an oath not to tell anyone of his death. Tied to his pledge Aubrey cannot prevent his sister from marrying the resurrected Ruthven a year later. The other male revenant, who hunted literary England in the mid-nineteenth century, was Francis Varney who, descended from a noble line, inflicts trouble on an entire family. However, he "displays remorse for his

---

[89] Bram Stoker, *Dracula*, eds. Nina Auerbach and David J. Skal (London: W.W. Norton & Company, 1997) 43. All quotes are taken from this edition, referred to as *Dracula* in the text.
[90] William Hughes, "Fictional Vampires in the Nineteenth and Twentieth Centuries," ed. David Punter, *A Companion to the Gothic* (Malden, Mass.: Blackwell Publishers Ltd., 2000) 146.
[91] Clive Leatherdale, *Dracula – The Novel & The Legend: A Study of Bram Stoker's Gothic Masterpiece* (Brighton: Desert Island Books, ²1993) 156.
[92] Its authorship is alternately attributed to James Malcolm Rymer or Thomas Preskett Prost.
[93] Tom Holland, "Undead Byron," *Byromania: Portraits of the Artist in Nineteenth- and Twentieth-Century Culture,* ed. Frances Wilson (London: Macmillian Press, 1999) 155.
[94] Cf. Ken Gelder, *Reading the Vampire* (London; New York: Routledge, 1994) 30.
[95] John Polidori, "The Vampyre; a Tale," *Children of the Night: Classic Vampire Stories*, ed. David Stuart Davies (London: Wordsworth Editions, 2007) 7. All quotes are taken from this edition, referred to as *The Vampyre* in the text.

bloodthirsty past and finally commits suicide by leaping into a volcano"[96] not able to bear his own further existence and, thus, leads the way for the more sympathetic, twentieth-century vampire.

The "male vampire of the nineteenth century has roots in the Gothic novel and Byron's villain-heroes"[97]. Stoker's Count Dracula, who became the prototype for the sanguivorous revenant[98], living in a palpable Gothic surrounding in the Carpathians is in regard to his physics a true Gothic villain. He is tall and "clad in black from head to foot" (*Dracula* 21) with a "very strong – aquiline" (*Dracula* 23) face; "his eyes blazed with a sort of demoniac fury" (*Dracula* 31) and looked as if "the flames of hell-fire blazed behind them" (*Dracula* 43). He, too, has the aura of mystery inherent to the Gothic villain as he is not the typical nobleman because he has "no servants in the house" (*Dracula* 32). Additionally, Stoker gives his villain some sense of melancholy and remorse in the words "I too can love; you yourselves can tell it from the past" (*Dracula* 43) which also leaves Dracula with an obscure past that is characteristic for the Gothic villain.

The nineteenth-century male vampire is always a nobleman, an aristocrat as much as the undead of the twentieth century is in general of higher social standing[99] such as Louis and Lestat from *The Vampire Chronicles*. Through their status in society male vampires depict aristocratic attributes of "Ausbeutung, Unterdrückung und erotischer Unersättlichkeit [um die] in der Vampirmythe angelegten Elemente des Parasitentums, der Gewalt und der Wollust zu veranschaulichen"[100]. Thus, the vampire could give a coded portrait of the decadent Victorian society as it dwells in it whereas, on the contrary, the female vampire mostly lingers at more seclusive places of human society. As the male vampire stands in the center of Victorian society, he penetrates it from within. He presents the internal threat a culture suffers from as he is "both an 'enemy within' and an externalised (or externalisable) fear"[101]. At the same time he epitomizes otherness and alienation at the heart of society, constructing a dichotomy between the self and the other defining one another.

---

[96] Margaret L Carter, „Revampings of Dracula in Contemporary Fiction," *Journal of Dracula Studies* Nr. 3 2001, 28.04.2010 <http://blooferland.com/drc/images/03Carter.rtf> 1.
[97] Carter, "The Vampire," *Icons of Horror and the Supernatural*, ed. S. T. Joshi, 622.
[98] Cf. Susanne Pütz, *Vampire und ihre Opfer: Der Blutsauger als literarische Figur* (Bielefeld: Aisthesis Verlag, 1992) 29-30.
[99] Cf. Hans Richard Brittnacher, *Ästhetik des Horrors: Gespenster, Vampire, Monster, Teufel und künstliche Menschen in der phantastischen Literatur* (Frankfurt am Main: Suhrkamp Verlag, 1994) 130.
[100] Ibid., 171.
[101] Hughes, "Fictional Vampires in the Nineteenth and Twentieth Centuries," ed. David Punter, *A Companion to the Gothic*, 148.

Probably no vampire forced a bigger threat on Victorian society than Dracula. With his otherness Stoker emblematizes the contrariness between human and non-human and turns the vampire into the prevailing evil it was already regarded as but not yet fully displayed in earlier vampire fiction. This revenant infiltrates cultural values of hierarchy and the family as well as established gender roles just as the female vampire does so that the destruction of it is necessary to maintain cultural norms[102]. His power is essentially in the threat that he as an overtly archaic subject poses to the modern world which needs to be protected. As such the vampire – "a symbol of taboo"[103] – again transgresses boundaries, not only of the self and the other or of desire and sexuality but also of the past and the present and of scientific progress demonstrating its capability and proving its constant popularity as "a multi-purpose monster"[104]. Nineteenth-century vampire stories treat topics such as "the breakdown of contemporary communities, of instability within the family, of the demise of religion as source of values and of strength"[105] presenting "the shortcomings of the Victorian cultural system"[106] that the vampire effectually allegorizes. As such it displays the intrusion of the archaic and its catalogue of obsolete norms and values into modern society threatening present-day social codes and beliefs.

---

[102] Brittnacher, *Ästhetik des Horrors*, 154.
[103] David Punter, *The Literature of Terror – A History of Gothic Fictions from 1765 to the present day. The Gothic Tradition, Volume I* (London; New York: Longman Group, [2]1996) 103.
[104] Paul Goetsch, *Monsters in English Literature: From the Romantic Age to the First World War* (Frankfurt am Main: Peter Lang Verlag, 2002) 15.
[105] Michael R. Collings, Dr, "Of Vampires and Their Ilk: Traditions, Transformations, and the UnDead," *The Unauthorized Anne Rice Companion,* ed. George Beahm (Kansas City, Mo.: Andrews and McMeel, 1996) 103.
[106] Richard Anderson, *"Dracula,* Monsters and the Apprehensions of Modernity," *Bram Stoker's Dracula: Sucking through the Century 1897-1997,* ed. Carol Margaret Davison (Toronto; Oxford: Dundurn Press, 1997) 324.

5. Intertextual Structures, Themes, and Characters in the *Twilight* Series

The ongoing popularity of Stephenie Meyer's *Twilight* saga which attracts readers of all age groups has led to a continuous debate within a scholarly context as well as in popular media. Meyer's apparent use of intertextual references throughout the series has been a frequent point of remark in interviews and articles on the series. Furthermore, works which she openly relies on in the construction of her stories are on the top of the list of her personal favorite books[107]. The assumption that Meyer, who majored in English at university, is familiar with certain characteristics of the Gothic novel, the Byronic hero, British Romanticism and the depiction of the literary vampire seems likely and is something she also acknowledges to some degree[108].

In this chapter, a closer look will be taken at the most important intertextual evidence detectable in the *Twilight* series. Thus, it will be necessary to focus on three distinct cornerstones of Meyer's work which appear to be of great intertextual significance for the formation of the novels: the figure of the postmodern vampire as it affects the ongoing development of the vampire archetype but nonetheless bears characteristics of its nineteenth-century predecessors up until the present day, the theme of the star-crossed lovers which is present throughout the entire series, as well as doubling figures and structures that intertextually wrap up the saga.

5.1. THE POSTMODERN VAMPIRE FIGURE

There is scarcely another figure among the rows of monsters in fantastic literature that has so many faces and undergone as many changes as the vampire. From aristocratic Gothic villain and bloodthirsty revenant to intimate friend and voluptuous *femme fatale*, the literary vampire has transgressed social and cultural boundaries. It has penetrated familial structures and gender roles just as vigorously as it has corrupted hierarchical orders of power in nineteenth-century Victorian England. As a liminal figure metaphorically coded in a number of ways its persistent appeal has even outlasted the twentieth century and gave it new impulses far

---

[107] Meyer cites Jane Austen, the Brontës, and William Shakespeare as a big influence on her writing in Stephenie Meyer, "Love at First Bite: Stephenie Meyer talks about vampires, teen love, and her first novel, 'Twilight'," Interview with Rick Margolis, *School Library Journal* 1 Oct. 2005, 1 Nov. 2010 <http://www.schoollibraryjournal.com/article/CA6260602.html>.

[108] "An Interview with Stephenie Meyer" (supplementary material on 2nd DVD). *Twilight: Biss zum Morgengrauen,* dir. Catherine Hardwicke, perfs. Robert Pattinson, Kristen Stewart, and Billy Burke, 2008, DVD, 2 Disc Fan Edition, Concorde Home Entertainment, 2009.

beyond its original outlook in British Romanticism. Clothed into the peculiarities of modernity the vampire has turned sympathetic as well as truly malicious, thus finally accommodating every angle of human understanding and perception.

The revenants in *Twilight* shed a new light on the coded nature of their own race as the heterogeneous types of vampires displayed in the tetralogy illustrate a wide range of characteristics of their nineteenth-century predecessors. As such, it will be of interest to take a closer look at how the postmodern vampire is constructed within an intertextual framework in the *Twilight* series. The shift in perspective in the series, ranging from ordinary human to peculiarly other, as well as Meyer's construction of the Byronic hero display a capability for intertextual potential. Her various depictions of the female vampire draw comparisons to earlier constructions of the vampiress. The representations of good and evil as well as the vampire's position in society are further points of great significance as they exemplify the creature's development towards its postmodern counterpart.

5.1.1. The Other Perspective

The other perspective has been immanent in fantastic literature and especially in the Gothic novel since Romanticism. When Mary Shelley gave her monster a voice in her debut Gothic masterpiece *Frankenstein* in 1818, it was particularly to level the reader's emphatic understanding for her monstrous character. The creature's tale that encloses the story of the lovers Felix De Lacey and Safie at the precise heart of the narration arouses the reader's sympathy. It makes its actions credible and comprehensible for the readers that would otherwise not grasp the monster's cruel and gory deeds. When Varney in the end of the penny-dreadful *Varney the Vampire* tells his story through his own eyes and eventually commits suicide as a form of self-punishment, he turns sympathetic and remorseful, thus forestalling later twentieth- and twenty-first-century literary vampires – a convention that Stoker, however, does not pick up on in *Dracula*. Nevertheless, it became a tendency that other writers of vampire stories like Fred Saberhagen or Anne Rice adopted in telling the vampire's tale from the revenant's perspective.

The case in *Twilight* appears slightly different. The story is told by a first-person-narrator who is simultaneously a character in the story and the protagonist of the four novels. Above all, Bella Swan, the heroine of the *Twilight* series, is human for the greatest part of the plot. The limited point of view the story is told from and the unreliable narration that is consistently evident throughout the series serve to further the sense of a more than human standpoint that is expressed since the reader would normally expect to encounter a heroine who would less embrace the other than Bella Swan apparently does[109].

However, Bella's description of her own position as a mere loner and outsider is telling. "I didn't relate well to people, period. [...] Sometimes I wondered if I was seeing the same things through my eyes that the rest of the world was seeing through theirs. Maybe there was a glitch in my brain"[110]. The distance and inability to relate to other human characters of the novel pervades the saga up until the point when Bella, on the verge of death, is finally transformed into a vampire herself. Even her best human friend Jacob, a shape-shifting werewolf, turns out not to be so ordinary after all. The protagonist obviously feels far more at home in the world of the fantastic than among the humans at school as "all this attention was annoying to Bella"[111]. Soon past her transmutation into a vampiress, after having beaten her stepbrother and fellow vampire Emmett in arm-wrestling, Bella observes her new vampire skin sparkle in the sunlight for the first time. She acknowledges: "It was like I had been born to be a vampire. [...] I had found my true place in the world, the place I fit, the place I shined."[112] Being a vampire is a state of being that evidently suits her far more than her previous existence as a human. By the time she is eventually transformed, all her acquaintances are somewhat dangerous superhumans, be it vampires or werewolves, while ordinary humans almost entirely disappear from her social circle. Due to her monstrous pregnancy even the contact to her father is more than marginal at that point.

Nevertheless, to narrate the plot from Bella's point of view gives the reader, in particular in the beginning, a human perspective on the events. It makes it easy to reconstruct Bella's actions and feelings. However, it also imparts an aura of mystery on Edward Cullen and the other vampires and makes them appear even more supernatural with their complexion that is "devastatingly, inhumanly beautiful" (*Twilight* 17) and their strange behavior. Bella's point of view is especially intelligible because she claims to be an "absolutely ordinary"

---

[109] Bella's rapid acceptance of her lover's otherness, her passivity but also her repeated worry about others have let many critics to regard her limitations as annoying rather than as a fictional device. Cf. Cotsirilos, "Bella and Byron," <http://www.hcs.harvard.edu/~hbr/main/current-issue/teresa-cotsirilos-bella-and-byron>.
[110] Stephenie Meyer, *Twilight* (London: Atom Books, 2007) 9-10. All quotes are taken from this edition, referred to as *Twilight* in the text.
[111] Stephenie Meyer, "Midnight Sun," *The Official Website of Stephenie Meyer*, 28 Aug. 2008, 1 Nov. 2010 <http://www.stepheniemeyer.com/pdf/midnightsun_partial_draft4.pdf> 103. All quotes are taken from this manuscript, referred to as *Midnight Sun* in the text.
[112] Stephenie Meyer, *Breaking Dawn* (London: Atom Books, 2008) 485. All quotes are taken from this edition, referred to as *Breaking Dawn* in the text.

(*Twilight* 184) girl in the beginning, a characteristic that is repeatedly stressed by means of unreliable narration and free indirect discourse throughout the series.

However, in spite of everything, she is not. Notwithstanding the threat Edward's vampiric nature poses to her, the narrator is fascinated by him and his animalistic attributes. She confesses that, while they are on the meadow for the first time and he shows her what he is capable of, she had "never seen him so completely freed of that carefully cultivated façade. He'd never been less human … or more beautiful" (*Twilight* 232). Furthermore, the vampire family captivates her and appeals to her "despite the natural aversion most humans felt toward the Cullens"[113]. The narrator's perspective is not characterized as an ordinary human perspective on the events and actions. It is determined by the attraction and the straightforward appeal the Cullens and the werewolves pose on the protagonist, an allurement that fellow humans do not exercise on Bella. Even Edward notes that Bella is truly different from her fellow humans claiming that she "must not think in the same way as other humans at all. That must be the explanation behind her mental silence. She was entirely other" (*Midnight Sun* 100). Additionally, although she never once articulates jealousy for Jacob's werewolf status, she strongly envies his ability to slow down his own aging process (*Eclipse* 106-107) which promises him an extended life span, probably far beyond an ordinary human life. She strongly wishes for an exceptional life which would suit her more than the life of an ordinary human.

Furthermore, the protagonist's fear of and for the other characterizes her ambivalent status between outsider and insider. She is never in fear of Edward Cullen whom she should be afraid of since he repeatedly acknowledges that he desires to drink her blood: "I was a vampire, and she had the sweetest blood I'd smelled in eighty years" (*Midnight Sun* 10). However, she fears for him and her shape-shifting best friend Jacob (*Eclipse* 341), and later on for her monstrous child repeatedly disregarding her own safety and will to survive. The heroine's excessive fear for other superhuman characters strengthens her position in having evoked a quite unusual perspective since "normal humans run away from monsters" (*Eclipse* 100) whereas she tries to shield the ones she feels attached to.

The narration is only in the beginning told from the perspective of a mere outsider. As the story is developed further the twofold status of the protagonist between normal human existence and successive supernatural life changes. The feeling of non-affiliation to other humans is a characteristic of the narrator that immediately draws her to the monsters of the

---

[113] Stephenie Meyer, *Eclipse* (London: Atom Books, 2007) 10. All quotes are taken from this edition, referred to as *Eclipse* in the text.

series. The perspective that Meyer achieves is not the perspective of an outsider but the development of a point of view that stands on a threshold to a mere inside perspective of the fantastic other since the possibility of an ordinary human life is from the start not taken into account. Through the protagonist's dissociation from other humans and her affection for her monstrous friends and later family-to-be Meyer accomplishes a perspective that is converted leading to a transformation of the self into an other via discovering one's own otherness. This makes her monsters mysterious as much as it offers the potential to create empathy for some of them.

The perspective that is given to the reader through the character of Jacob Black is somewhat different. As a shape-shifting werewolf he is a direct opponent to the vampires of *Twilight* in general because their appearance triggered his transformation into a werewolf[114] (*Eclipse* 106), a state of being that he initially despises. His position as a narrator, particularly in *Breaking Dawn*, holds the status of an I-as-witness. He stands at the periphery of events and cannot influence the main actions that take place at that point of the narration. Bella's determination to deliver her baby (*Breaking Dawn* 180) leaves him helpless just like Edward's decision to change Bella after accouchement or die: "The moment Bella's heart stops beating, I will be begging for you to kill me" (*Breaking Dawn* 168). Through his incapability to intervene he is a mere outsider, not fully understanding the protagonists' actions. In his position as an outsider and I-as-witness he shares characteristics with the two principal narrators of Emily Brontë's *Wuthering Heights*[115]. However, Jacob's perspective is still different in that he himself is, although not vampiric, supernatural and incorporates the other. Although he is still human as he notes himself (*Eclipse* 99), he is as abnormal as Edward and can provide the reader with a different point of view on the saga's vampires.

The perspective of the other is also applied in the *Twilight* series. Through the adoption of various sequences of analepses throughout the course of the saga (*Twilight* 289-90, 390-91, *Eclipse* 138-46, 256-68) a glint of limited perspective of the most consistent vampire characters, namely the Cullens, is observable. As such, their motivations and personalities are rendered comprehensible. This is especially the case with Rosalie whose

---

[114] Cf. Stephenie Meyer, *New Moon* (London: Atom Books, 2006) 272. All quotes are taken from this edition, referred to as *New Moon* in the text.
[115] Cf. Emily Brontë, *Wuthering Heights* (London: Penguin Books, 1994). Lockwood, the new tenant of Thrushcross Grange, and Nelly Dean, a servant to each generation of the two families at both houses, narrate the story as bystanders, as I-as-witnesses. They are both unreliable in their recount of events and just as Jacob they do not comprehend the characters' actions to the fullest. Lockwood misinterprets Heathcliff's behavior already on their first encounter claiming that "I know, by instinct, his reserve springs from an aversion to showy displays of feeling" (*Wuthering Heights* 21) – just to rectify his own impressions a second later: "I bestow my own attributes over liberally on him" (*Wuthering Heights* 21).

wish to have a family and simply live a long and happy, even if temporally limited, life explains her motivation to dislike Bella in the beginning and to protect Renesmee against all odds: "Blondie would be in line with anything that helped the little life-sucking monster" (*Breaking Dawn* 221). A fuller rendition of such a perspective is given in Meyer's manuscript *Midnight Sun* and also in the recently published *The Short Second Life of Bree Tanner – An Eclipse Novella*. Narrated from Edward's point of view *Midnight Sun* gives the reader a full understanding of Edward's actions in the first part of the series. The vampiric perspective that is presented removes his aura of mystery, makes his deeds comprehensible and unveils his motivation in keeping Bella alive and not turning her into a vampire. According to this, the impression that everyone in the series acts reasonably emerges due to narrations from the other perspective.

The effect that is achieved through a first-person-narration with Edward's point of view is a far more effective construction of the vampire's psyche than through Bella's perspective. The depiction of a vampire's inner life results in a, as Gordon and Hollinger entitled it, "domestication"[116] of the other. The supernatural is examined and can be clearly defined and the vampire lifestyle now seems more like a different way of life than something thoroughly other. What would normally seem foreign and could provoke horror and angst is rationally depicted. Through the inside perspective terror is diminished by what otherwise would remain outside of the familiar and known sphere. As a technique that has obviously been quite prominent in vampire literature since the 1970s as Anne Rice and other writers of vampire fiction apply it just as easily as Meyer does, it is also an approach that already Mary Shelley makes in her Gothic novel *Frankenstein*.

Shelley's novel which is told through a number of frame narratives and places the monster's tale structurally at the heart of the story also uses first-person-narration to recount the Creature's life story. The motivation of the Creature to tell its tale is to persuade Frankenstein to create a fellow female creature for it so that it can "quit for ever [sic] the neighbourhood of man, and lead a harmless life"[117]. The story it then tells is the tale of its repudiation by society. Treated as an outcast from the earliest moments of its existence it is first disowned by its creator and later on by the family it helps unobserved and secretly to sustain their lives. People who see it react with "horror and consternation" (*Frankenstein* 91)

---

[116] Joan Gordon and Veronica Hollinger, "Introduction: The Shape of Vampires," *Blood Read: The Vampire as Metaphor in Contemporary Culture*, eds. Joan Gordon and Veronica Hollinger (Philadelphia: University of Pennsylvania Press, 1997) 2.
[117] Mary Shelley, *Frankenstein*, ed. J. Paul Hunter (New York: W.W. Norton & Company, 1996) 67. All quotes are taken from this edition, referred to as *Frankenstein* in the text.

to its inhuman looks and immense stature. The Creature's violent reactions towards the De Lacey family which it tries to befriend and to humans it accidentally comes across later on are determined by the repeated repudiation and antipathy it encounters. However, it is precisely this refusal through human society that triggers sympathy for the Creature in the reader apart from the monster's own characterization that links him to the fictional Werther: "I applied much personally to my own feeling and condition. I found myself similar" (*Frankenstein* 86).

Just as the Creature's tale in Mary Shelley's *Frankenstein* provokes sympathy in the reader it also expands the circle of destruction around itself by telling its own tale. The Creature's recount of how it killed Frankenstein's brother William and laid the blame on the innocent girl Justine (*Frankenstein* 97) even enlarges its guilt. This deed is rendered more monstrous and gory when told directly by the wrongdoer who blames "the sanguinary laws of man" (*Frankenstein* 97) to have made it a monster in character. The same holds true for Edward Cullen. Already through Bella's perspective it becomes obvious that Edward follows her in order to protect her. However, the sheer enormity of his obsession with her and her safety is not fully revealed until one looks at his narration of the events. He does not only stalk her during her shopping trip in Port Angeles but also watches her from a tree in front of her house (*Midnight Sun* 160-62) while she is reading a Jane Austen novel (*Twilight* 128). The climax of his infatuation is reached when he actually penetrates her private sphere by entering her bed-room through the window at night without her knowledge and watching her sleep – a scene that culminates in Edward's own comment on his behavior: "How was I any better than some sick peeping tom? I *wasn't* any better. I was much, much worse" (*Midnight Sun* 106). In addition, this violation of Bella's privacy is epitomized by his calculations of bringing oil along to fix her window frame the next time he intrudes into her room (*Midnight Sun* 107, 153). As such, Edward's obsession with the series' female protagonist takes on a far more compulsive dimension from the vampire's point of view, similar to Mary Shelley's delineation of the Creature's tale.

The presentation of the other through a shift in perspective is intertextual. First adopted as a still unconventional technique by Shelley, the narration with the focus on the other is commonly used today. Meyer positions her series in the tradition and progression of contemporary vampire fiction by adopting a perspective that does not regard the vampire as a mere outsider to what is familiar and known. She also aspires to modernize the concept of the other perspective by bestowing a voice to a human girl who feels not associated with other humans but would rather become a vampire herself. With the help of Bella Swan's narrative voice the world is still seen through human eyes but is close enough to the other to achieve a perspective that presents the unknown as uniquely sympathetic.

Eventually, Meyer's *Twilight* series is structurally intertextual concerning the aspect of perspective. Especially the narrative voices of Jacob as an I-as-witness and Edward as the other that are predominantly applied in *Breaking Dawn* and *Midnight Sun* have been existent before. Furthermore, the analepses of the Cullens' past that are woven into the saga have features in common with Shelley's *Frankenstein* because they are also framed within the series and are, thus, structurally intertextual. However, since the bigger part of the novels is narrated from the heroine's point of view with a unique perspective that is intermediary between human and non-human, Meyer employs an innovative point of view that has not been used by her predecessors.

5.1.2. Edward Cullen: a Postmodern Byronic Hero

The Byronic hero has spawned a number of prominent descendants over the past two hundred years – among them the prototypical character of Manfred developed by Byron, Charlotte Brontë's enigmatic Edward Rochester and Emily Brontë's devilish and vindictive Heathcliff to whom Meyer on occasion refers to in the intertextual construction of her hero. All of them handed down characteristics to twentieth-century incarnations of the Byronic hero. Atara Stein labels quite a few action heroes such as Eric Draven from the movie *The Crow*, Louis and Lestat from Rice's *The Vampire Chronicles*, the Terminator from the homonymous movie series as well as Angel from the TV series *Buffy – The Vampire Slayer* as modern-day representations of this nineteenth-century hero type. As such, already several literary and cinematic vampire figures have adopted Byronic qualities so that it inevitably seems that Byronic characteristics are tailor-made for them to express their otherness and transitional nature.

Meyer's vampiric hero, Edward Cullen, whom she named after *Jane Eyre*'s Edward Rochester[118] and whose last name at birth, Masen (*New Moon* 34), homophonically resembles *Jane Eyre*'s mentally disturbed Bertha Mason[119], stands in the line of this popular hero type.

---

[118] Cotsirilos, "Bella and Byron," < http://www.hcs.harvard.edu/~hbr/main/current-issue/teresa-cotsirilos-bella-and-byron>.
[119] Kate Cochran already points this out in her essay on Edward's literary past. Cochran, "'An Old-Fashioned Gentleman'?", 16.

Just like the Byronic heroes who precede him he is already extraordinary in his physical complexion, startling and dazzling other humans with his appearance. Everything about him is pictured as exceedingly beautiful and mesmerizing and Meyer's description of his physics is strongly recurrent. His face is "dazzling" (*Twilight* 37) and every single feature of it is frequently alluded to as "perfect" (*Twilight* 16, 18, 43, 46, 146) or "too-perfect" (*Twilight* 63). His inhuman beauty makes him look like "a Greek god" (*Twilight* 180) who has just "finished shooting a commercial for hair gel" (*Twilight* 37). What especially marks him are his eyes that are either topaz (*New Moon* 8, *Breaking Dawn* 605, 670) or black (*Twilight* 20, 62) which have a "devastating power" (*Twilight* 49) over Bella but could also burn "with the intensity of the thirst he fought" (*New Moon* 29). Additionally, his voice is depicted as musical, appealing, velvet, and like melting honey (*Twilight* 37, 52, 70, 88) as if he has "the voice of an archangel" (*Twilight* 272). What also singles him out for Bella is his breathtaking crooked smile (*Twilight* 76) which is also referred to as being "a gentle angel's smile" (*Twilight* 298). Another characteristic that is repeatedly turned to in the series is the texture of his skin which is pale, icy (*Twilight* 193) and "carved from […] stone" (*Twilight* 153) but at the same time "smooth white" (*Twilight* 224) and "literally sparkled, like thousands of tiny diamonds" (*Twilight* 228) in the sun. Furthermore, his body is described as being "a perfect statue" and "a carving of Adonis" (*Twilight* 228, 261), thus evoking comparisons that confer a status to Edward which situates his outward appearance in the proximity of Greek depictions of beauty. Even his scent invites Bella in because it is "sweet, delicious, the scent made my mouth water" (*Twilight* 230).

Byron's Manfred, the prototypical Byronic hero, is of similarly striking appearance as his clothes are "goodly, his mien manly, and his air / Proud as a free-born peasant's"[120] who is also "of high lineage– / One of the many chiefs, whose castled crags" (*Manfred* II.1.7-9). While Manfred is presented as being aristocratic, Edward as a postmodern Byronic hero is depicted as being well off and thus "money meant next to nothing to Edward or the rest of the Cullens" (*New Moon* 12). This is a characteristic that is handed down from the Gothic villain as also Dracula notes the great significance of his lineage whom he refers to as "a conquering race" (*Dracula* 34). However, noticeable about Manfred is also the potency of "the most seeming virtuous eye" (*Manfred* I.1.244) that is inherent in all men that are associated with the Byronic hero type. Nevertheless, Byron does not dwell on his hero's looks as much as

---

[120] Lord George Gordon Byron, "Manfred," *The Norton Anthology of English Literature 8th Edition: The Romantic Period*, eds. Jack Stillinger and Deidre Shauna Lynch (New York: W.W. Norton & Company, 2006) I.2.62-64. All quotes are taken from this edition, referred to as *Manfred* in the text.

Stephenie Meyer, or as Emily Brontë does in the depiction of her villain-hero, Heathcliff. Lockwood sees in him "a dark-skinned gypsy in aspect, in dress and manner a gentleman" (*Wuthering Heights* 21), a dichotomy between appearance and behavior that shows Lockwood's unreliability in his narration and puts Brontë's hero in an in-between position – a status that he carries with himself for the entire narrative. However, also young Heathcliff is characterized as being "a dirty, ragged, black-haired child" (*Wuthering Heights* 45) whose origins are shrouded in obscurity and who continuously stays a mystery for the narrators of the story. His character traits and outward appearance single him out along with his "eyes deep-set and singular" (*Wuthering Heights* 90) among the inhabitants of Wuthering Heights and Thrushcross Grange. Similarly, Rochester's features, although initially not handsome, are depicted as strikingly peculiar on Jane's first encounter with him as he has "a dark face, with stern features and a heavy brow"[121]. With his "decisive nose, more remarkable for character than beauty; [...] his grim mouth, chin, and jaw" (*Jane Eyre* 121) already his appearance is mysterious. Moreover, his character is presented as particularly brooding as his vespertine conversations with Jane show.

Edward, too, appears to be shrouded in mystery to Bella's eyes while other humans repeatedly regard the Cullens as mere freaks (*Midnight Sun* 77, 131, 158, 258). His behavior towards the heroine initially swinging from complete disregard to protective care is inapprehensible to her as much as it is to him (*Midnight Sun* 31). As a Byronic hero he repeatedly dwells in a constant mixture of guilt for his past and present sins which is only heightened by his self-assurance to take away Bella's opportunity to live a normal life as long as he stays near her. His steady remorse for the constant dangers he puts her in is what Gothic villain and Hero of Sensibility conflate into one another in the character of Edward Cullen. His grief over the repulsion that he believes Bella to nourish over his monstrousness further enforces this sense of guilt and remorse: "I was a monster. How could she see me as anything else? If she knew the truth about me [...] Like the intended victim in a horror movie, she would run away, shrieking in terror" (*Midnight Sun* 108). Edward's remorse over the dangers to which he exposes her go from fully-fledged self-hatred – "my very existence puts you at risk. Sometimes I truly hate myself. I should be stronger, I should be able to [leave]" (*Twilight* 319) – to the act of completely abandoning Bella to give her "a chance at a normal, happy, human life" (*New Moon* 452) which furthermore intensifies the Byronic characteristic of guilt and remorse in him.

---

[121] Charlotte Brontë, *Jane Eyre* (London: Penguin Books, 1994) 115. All quotes are taken from this edition, referred to as *Jane Eyre* in the text.

The character of Edward Cullen presents some truly Byronic qualities to the reader. His aura of mystery constantly surrounds him as long as the narrator, Bella Swan, has not reached her own level of superhumanity which uncloaks Edward's mysterious behavior later on. Adopted from the Gothic villain his mysteriousness is a trait that enhances his affiliation to the fantastic and fosters his otherness. This is already apparent in Stoker's *Dracula* in which the vampiric villain remains without a voice for the most part of the narrative as he is simply reduced to a menace the protagonists have to face. Accordingly, Dracula only appears as a threat triggering the other characters' reactions to his deeds. Similarly, Rochester's past appears mysterious as not even his housekeeper knows what the "painful position" (*Jane Eyre* 129) is he is in because of his father and his brother's doings. Cloaked into mystery is also Edward's sense of guilt for neither being able to offer Bella an ordinary human life in the beginning nor being capable enough to protect her. It is precisely this sense of guilt that leads him into leaving his beloved in *New Moon*. This sense of guilt is already inherent in Byron's hero Manfred whose feelings of indebtedness due to Astarte's mysterious death arouse his "fierce thirst of death" (*Manfred* II.1.48).

Notwithstanding Edward's wish to offer Bella a normal life, he does not completely condemn his vampiric existence. He actually enjoys the physical strength he gains through it as much as he benefits from his mind-reading capability. His sense of superiority is immanent and surfaces frequently with reference to humans that he regards as inferior because "beyond protecting … [his] family from suspicion, human thoughts were not significant" (*Midnight Sun* 44) and neither are humans to him. Other men are "sheep-like males" (*Midnight Sun* 1) to him and his repeated intrusion into others' minds, a skill that already Anne Rice endows her fictional vampires in *The Vampire Chronicles* with[122], arms him with a strong enough sense of abasement towards the trivial thoughts of his fellow students. Furthermore, he enjoys frightening humans at times. Thence, he is irritated to find out that he has lost some of that potential due to his feelings for Bella: "It was […] a bit embarrassing…to realize how much being near Bella had softened me. It seemed like no one was afraid of me any more [sic]" (*Midnight Sun* 223).

His sense of superiority and his otherness also turn him into a fully-fledged outsider – a misfit as all the previous Byronic heroes in manifold ways. He is singled out from humans by his vampiric nature which is underlined by the difference in looks from humans. Also as a vampire he is particular in that he and his family stay abstinent from human blood but rather

---

[122] Lestat describes his ability to hear other mortals' thoughts during his first awakening as a vampire in Anne Rice, *The Vampire Lestat: Book II of The Vampire Chronicles* (New York: Ballantine Books, 1993) 109.

feed on animals. They are expelled from human society due to their undead state of being and the deviance from ordinary humans. However, they are also regarded as a rarity in the supernatural world of *Twilight* due to their human-free blood consumption as it is for other vampires "*abnormal* for so many [...] to live together in peace" (*New Moon* 377-78). Moreover, Edward's outsider status entails not only societal but also personal consequences for himself. At the beginning of the series, he is the only one in the Cullen coven who has not found someone to spend eternity with, which furthermore facilitates his brooding nature (*Midnight Sun* 56).

Byronic heroes are generally either outsiders or outcasts to society. Manfred is an outsider in his position among fellow humans. His thirst for knowledge and his capabilities as a magus – characteristics that are bestowed on him by the Faustian hero – elevate him to a status which is above ordinary people. He is "not of thine order" (*Manfred* II.1.38), a state that seems plain to him and that he dismisses. His denial of affiliation to other humans resembles Edward's superiority towards his fellow students. Similarly, Manfred's status as an outsider is twofold. As much as he differentiates himself in power from the Chamois Hunter and the Abbot, who function as representatives of the laboring and the ecclesiastical classes, he still cannot achieve the forgetfulness he truly desires. Although he transgresses the boundaries of human powers and can command spirits, he cannot decide on his own to end his life. Just as the eternal Wanderer he is bound to live, depending on higher powers to grant him oblivion in death. Comparably, Rochester is displayed as an outsider as he is on the one hand unable to marry the woman he desires but is bound to his mentally ill first wife and on the other hand only accepted by his invited party and in particular Blanche Ingram because he is rich.

Meanwhile, Edward's contemptuous treatment of others results from his mind-reading ability as well as his being a vampire which makes him more powerful than others. However, this Byronic sense of superiority is already represented in the character of Manfred. He disregards the spirits he summoned himself and disobeys the Witch of the Alps:

> I will not swear–Obey! and whom? the spirits /
> Whose presence I command, and be the slave /
> Of those who served me–Never! (*Manfred* II.2.158-60)

Along with this goes a strict defiance of authority that culminates in Manfred's rejection of the Abbot's wishes which originates in his extraordinariness that was handed down to the Byronic hero from the Noble Outlaw.

This is a state that Edward shares with Manfred. Just as Byron's hero, he is pledged to immortality and an eternal existence due to the near invulnerability of the vampiric body which can hardly be destroyed (*New Moon* 16-17). However, Manfred, no matter how doomed he is, does not wish to exchange his life for an ordinary life, which is what Edward, although only due to his love for Bella, desires: "If there were any way for me to become human for you – no matter what the price was, I would pay it" (*Eclipse* 242). Humanity is what he envies other humans for and what causes in him distress since it is the greatest distinction between them: "I didn't want to look at Bella and myself side by side in the sunlight. The difference between us was already insurmountable" (*Midnight Sun* 161). Due to Bella's mortality Edward's inability to age poses a problem to their relationship that can only be solved by Bella's transformation in the end. The same boundary of life and death also forms a tremendous challenge for Heathcliff and Cathy's relationship so that he creates a strong belief in being haunted by her ghost in order to live on in the subsequent years after her death. An almost as insurmountable problem is addressed in Brontë's *Jane Eyre* where the protagonists are not only unable to consume their love but are only ready for reunion when the balance in their relationship is restored. Consequently, Jane's inheritance, the burning down of Thornfield and Rochester's partially only temporary injuries function to eventually counterbalance their relationship.

Heathcliff's outsider status is repeatedly brought up in Hindley and Edgar's behavior towards him. He is degraded to work as a servant and he is frequently mocked by them. However, he manages to become somewhat wealthy in his three-year-absence and is capable of transcending class barriers and, eventually, becomes the owner of both houses. Just like Manfred's, Heathcliff's inherent existence as a societal outsider is twofold. He neither fills the role of a servant as he was brought up with Cathy and Hindley nor is he a common middle class proprietor. On that account, his obscured origin and appearance always depicts his non-affiliation to other characters.

Linked to his sense of superiority Meyer's Edward is thoroughly authoritative in his attitude towards others. He repeatedly berates Bella disapprovingly, for example for her dislike for attending her own graduation party or celebrating her birthday, by requiring from her not to be "too difficult" (*New Moon* 21) about the things she detests. Additionally, he is exceedingly protective and patronizing towards her, initially not letting her make her own decisions or ignoring her wishes when she wants to see Jacob (*Eclipse* 24-30). More than that, he consciously tries to manipulate her by attempting to "dazzle Bella on purpose" (*Midnight*

Sun 260) if she is not going along with his ways. This eventually culminates in his obsessive behavior in following her around and observing her sleep which also turns into a manifestly possessive behavior: "he replied [...] 'Bring on the shackles – I'm your prisoner.' But his long hands formed manacles around *my* wrists as he spoke" (*Twilight* 264). The paradox that is displayed in this scene emphasizes Edward's obsession with the heroine as he is entirely unable to leave her alone independent of her own will and wishes.

Meyer's hero also acts superior towards the shape-shifting Jacob whom he regards as a dog (*Eclipse* 29) and he sees werewolves in general as "immature, volatile, the worst thing out there besides Victoria herself" (*New Moon* 446). Moreover, the constant rivalry between Edward and Jacob for the heroine's love results in Edward's strong dislike for the werewolf and leads to the development of an understanding for the "devilish" (*Wuthering Heights* 152) Heathcliff on Edward's side: "I'm discovering that I can sympathize with Heathcliff in ways I didn't think possible before" (*Eclipse* 235). The intertextual link, thus created, endows Meyer's vampiric hero with another characteristic that affiliates him with the oppressive and passionate Heathcliff who would also "love and hate, equally under cover" (*Wuthering Heights* 21). Consequently, he looks down on ordinary humans, as well.

Edward too shows a great repudiation of rules. Just as Brontë's Heathcliff who falls in love with a woman of higher social status, Edward commits a crime against nature by loving a human girl and acknowledges that "I'm breaking *all* the rules now" (*Twilight* 174). Not only is his love for Bella unnatural but he also breaks a crucial rule enforced by the Volturi by inducting Bella into the specifics of his vampiric existence. His love is the reason why "rules no longer mattered" (*Midnight Sun* 206). Just as Edward, Heathcliff defies every authority and rule. His love for Cathy is illicit and his intrusion into her marriage with Edgar goes against social conventions.

Edward's disregard for an authority that he initially obeys because he "used to be the responsible one" (*Midnight Sun* 161) springs from his feelings for Bella. His Promethean rebellion goes, however, more against the nature of the universe and the order of things than against society in general. Edward's insurgence against society is collective, a divergence shared with his family members against predetermined ideas of how they as vampires should be and should live. This rebellion against societal rules appears to be the cornerstone of Edward's rebellion against the natural order which he disturbs by falling in love with a human. Thus, a Romantic tendency towards strong individualism that characterizes Edward in his position as an outsider is achieved. This radical drift towards individualism is also inherent in Manfred and Heathcliff, aided through their status as outsiders.

An essential characteristic of the Byronic hero is his expression of feelings and his strong passions which are features that he has inherited from the eighteenth-century Man of Feeling. Edward's feelings are almost exclusively bound to Bella and his family. His feelings are extremely passionate, make him obsessive, and they are irreversible. What differentiates him from the Man of Feeling is that he does not adopt his explicit whimsicalness and weak constitution and he, initially, has no interest in the concerns of other people besides the above mentioned. He only wants to do Angela Weber a favor "for simply being a nice person. It made me feel better to think that Bella had one friend worth having" (*Midnight Sun* 159). While Edward does not care for other humans' concerns over the preceding years of his existence his love for Bella changes him fundamentally and makes him compassionate (*Midnight Sun* 214-15). His determination to prevent other females from being harassed by the rapist and murderer who almost got a hold of Bella in Port Angeles shows his sudden concern for humans since "either one of them might be somebody's Bella" (*Midnight Sun* 212). However, he is, in general, courteous towards women, a characteristic he adopted from the Noble Outlaw, and has a great interest in music that links him again to this eighteenth-century hero type.

Edward turns even more into a modern-day Man of Feeling after Bella's transformation into a vampire which evens out their relationship and turns him fully sympathetic and feeling. He finds his place within their relationship and does no longer patronize his beloved. Similarly passionate in their love concerns are also Manfred and Heathcliff though they do not care about others like Edward does. Heathcliff is further turned disagreeable by his rude behavior towards women such as his wife Isabel who believed him to be "a hero of romance, and expecting unlimited indulgences from [...] chivalrous devotion" (*Wuthering Heights* 135). Furthermore, he also presents an unwelcoming attitude towards visitors like Lockwood to Wuthering Heights, thus displaying his indifference for others.

Manfred's claim for Astarte's love is not accomplished through her sudden death in which he took a hand. Likewise, Heathcliff and Cathy's all-consuming love for one another cannot be lived out freely outside their childhood reveries at Wuthering Heights. Only Heathcliff's death finally gives them the possibility for full reunion beyond the limits of earthly life. Thus, what often remains denied to the Romantic Byronic hero is the fulfillment of his love concerns in daily life. Neither Manfred nor Heathcliff are able to achieve this while they are still alive and also Rochester and Jane have to overcome a number of obstacles and accept limitations to finally be together. Yet Edward as a modern-day Byronic hero is granted this form of happy ending. Bella's final transformation into a vampire rehumanizes Edward and puts their relationship into a balance it did not have before. Consequently, Edward not only loses his constant aura of mystery but he is also rehumanized through Bella's perspective. The focus in *Breaking Dawn* eventually shifts completely from an ordinary human world to a depiction of the fantastic.

Meyer not only creates her own Byronic hero but also embeds into her tetralogy a number of features that were already productive in British Romanticism. The lovers' meadow, "the loveliest place I had ever seen" (*Twilight* 226), is a *locus amoenus* – a topos that was already prominent in antiquity – as it is depicted as immensely beautiful with "the bubbling music of a stream" (*Twilight* 226) and "a haze of buttery sunshine" (*Twilight* 227). Contrary to the meadow, the baseball clearing functions as a *locus terribilis* for games and fights as the main conflicts of the series are carried out in the clearing. But also the author's depictions of nature and the dichotomy she establishes between rural and urban life are reminders of Romanticism.

Meyer intertextually accomplishes to create a Byronic hero that incorporates all the essential Byronic qualities of his nineteenth-century forebears as he displays a deep sense of guilt, remorse as well as profound, irreversible feelings for his beloved. Nevertheless, the postmodern Byronic hero still has the capability for rehumanization that is denied to his predecessors. This modification makes him truly sympathetic in the end – a characteristic that is disavowed to Manfred and Heathcliff and that Rochester only achieves by being injured. Edward is de-Byronized in the course of the *Twilight* series, obtaining the reader's full empathy while successfully negotiating the transition from arrogant outcast to rather congenial vampire hero. The interfigurality that Meyer achieves between Manfred, Heathcliff, Rochester, and Edward is significant since Edward not only bears the name of one of the most influential Romantic Byronic heroes but also incorporates the most considerable Byronic qualities. This intertextual identification with former examples of this hero type leads to the diminishment of certain character traits while other attributes like the intensity of Edward's feelings and his sense of superiority are reinforced. The tension that is created between Edward and his forebears which is further stimulated through Edward's direct reference in his sympathies for Heathcliff and Rochester as his namesake is strongly intertextual.

5.1.3. The Female Vampire

Constricted to the two extremes of intimate friendship and erotic seduction the female vampire of the nineteenth century inhabited a grand range of metaphorical potential for examination. However, the female vampire was never provided with the capability to express more than either one of these two facets of closeness in this dichotomy. Whereas Le Fanu's *Carmilla*, Keats's *Lamia* and Coleridge's *Christabel* depict caring and loving female creatures despite their otherness, Coleridge's *The Rime of the Ancient Mariner* shows a woman that is apparently horrific and scary in her own otherness. They are only outplayed by Stoker's female seductresses who are radically presented as highly sexual and child-devouring women. Accordingly, Meyer had a great variety of vampiric predecessors to rely on in the construction of her own female vampires and, in fact, she created them using a wide assortment of characteristics that were already immanent in earlier accounts of fantastic female creatures.

The first female vampire that Bella gets to know is Edward's sister Alice who has the supernatural gift of seeing visions of the future. Physically, Alice is like Edward excruciatingly beautiful with her pixie-like "exquisite, elfin face" and her "willowy, graceful" stature. Furthermore, her voice is "almost as attractive as his" (*Twilight* 216) and its sound is "all silver, a wind chime" (*New Moon* 9). Her movements are repeatedly compared to a dancer's motions as she walks "in a fashion that would break any ballerina's heart" (*Twilight* 303) with "her lithe dancer's step" (*Twilight* 17). Meyer increasingly uses such allusions with reference to Alice to underline her physical delicateness which is only perfunctory and juxtaposes her corporal strength and superhuman abilities. Soon after their acquaintance Bella and Alice become friends and she is also the first of the female Cullens to show amicable intimacy with Bella through a kiss on the cheek (*Twilight* 283). She respects Bella's will and autonomy more than Edward does although she, at times, keeps her hostage on Edward's demand. However, she never objects to Bella's wish to become an immortal herself and Alice's suggestion to transform Bella by her own powers (*New Moon* 384) is a gesture of true companionship and compassion. She wants her brother to be happy as much as she wants to keep Bella eternally as a friend.

The friendship and companionship that Alice offers to the heroine cannot be compared to the intimacy that Carmilla and Laura share in Le Fanu's vampire novel which overtly transports homosexual sentiments. Meyer's series is in contrast blatantly free of such sensations. Yet Meyer's female vampires also have the capacity to affect humans by their inhuman beauty just as Geraldine bedazzles Christabel's father in Coleridge's fragmentary poem. When Alice and Bella race for Volterra to stop Edward from committing suicide she beguiles a flight attendant (*New Moon* 383) and a guard, "who wished he had better news for the strikingly beautiful woman", on purpose aided by her "alluring smile" (*New Moon* 393). Not surprisingly the friendly relationship that she entertains with Bella's father, Charlie, is not entirely free of such allurements as she tricks him with an "expression so devastated that Charlie leaned toward her automatically, one hand reaching out, looking for some way to help" (*Eclipse* 377) into letting Bella spend the weekend at the Cullen's. Charlie is "crazy about Alice" (*New Moon* 20) but also because she has been a great friend to Bella. The role that Alice takes up in the series is the position of the close friend to whom Meyer denies intimacy with the heroine. Instead this intimacy between human and the undead is acted out by Edward who takes up a characteristic that is in the history of vampire fiction originally linked to the female vampire.

Meanwhile, Esme with her "heart-shaped face" (*New Moon* 28) – an attribute that Meyer also endows on Bella (*Midnight Sun* 4) probably already suggesting her good qualities as a mother-to-be – enacts the position of the loving mother, as already her name suggests[123]. She "brought her ability to love passionately" (*Twilight* 269) in the family and acts motherly towards the other Cullens which further evokes a strong contrast to Bella's mother Renée, who impersonates the absent mother. More than that Esme also worries about Jacob and his pack of werewolves, thus triggering similar sentiments of his own mother in Jacob: "something about her expression suddenly reminded me of my mom" (*Breaking Dawn* 260). Her position is further epitomized in the story of her transformation. Losing her newborn baby is "why I jumped off the cliff" (*Twilight* 321). What Esme symbolizes is an inversion of the vampiress as a child-devouring monster as it is presented in Stoker's *Dracula*. The presentation of Esme is linked to the mythological Lamia who is initially a loving woman and only turned into a serpent-like monster that eats her own children through the envy of the goddess Hera. The intimacy that the female vampire embodies in nineteenth-century literature is also immanent in its contemporary successors although only on the layer of motherly love.

Alice as well as Esme is contrasted through Rosalie Hale. Just as all the Cullens Rosalie is inhumanly beautiful and her name which is derived from "rose" further underlines that notion. However, her beauty further exceeds her family members' complexion which is repeatedly marked by Meyer. Rosalie is "the incarnation of pure beauty" (*Twilight* 265), has a "divine face" (*New Moon* 27) and is "the most beautiful person on the planet" (*Eclipse* 148),

---

[123] Esme means "esteemed" or "loved" in Old French.

further emphasized by the often attention-grabbing outfits she wears. Even Jacob is full of "unwilling admiration as he tried to come up with a word to describe Edward's sister" (*Eclipse* 94-95). At the same time she shows open dislike towards Bella, glaring at her with her "dark, cold eyes" (*Twilight* 215) as she envies her for her humanity and for Edward's attention. She is repeatedly described as being vain and only focused on her own beauty: "She'd caught sight of her profile […] and she was mulling over her own perfection. Rosalie's mind was a shallow pool with few surprises" (*Midnight Sun* 1). With Emmett she has an intense relationship that is pictured as emotional (*Midnight Sun* 56) as much as it is sexual.

However, Rosalie also displays other features that clearly mark her as a *femme fatale*. Despite her unearthly beauty, her strong temperament and her animosity for Bella, which are likewise characteristics of the *femme fatale*, she turns out to be near fatal to Edward since her phone call triggers his attempt at getting killed by the Volturi. Meyer strongly marks that Rosalie acted as a *femme fatale* in the past through the analepsis she deploys to narrate Rosalie's former life in Rochester[124] (*Midnight Sun* 82) that preceded her transformation into a vampire. Dressed as a bride she delivers death to her former fiancé: "I was overly theatrical. It was kind of childish, really. I wore a wedding dress I'd stolen for the occasion. He screamed when he saw me. He screamed a lot that night" (*Eclipse* 146). Rosalie clearly has the capacity to act as a *femme fatale* and actually proves to be fatal to the man she was supposed to marry and his friends. Nevertheless, she does not take up the role of the vindictive demonic seductress again after this act of revenge and her interferences into Edward and Bella's relationship are mere acts of jealousy rather than revengeful deeds. Still, out of all the female Cullen vampires Rosalie gets closest to the archetype of the *femme fatale* that is already displayed in Keats's *Lamia* or Coleridge's *Christabel*. However, her fatality with Edward's suicide attempt is unconscious and unintended.

To find a fully-fledged *femme fatale* it is necessary to look outside of the Cullen family. Although only a minor character and of marginal importance for the story the female vampire Heidi represents all the important major characteristics of a demonic seductress. She is extraordinarily beautiful like Rosalie "though they looked nothing alike – it was just that her beauty, too, was exceptional, unforgettable" (*New Moon* 425). She dresses in red, tight

---

[124] Although a popular place name Meyer's choice to let Rosalie's revengeful act as a *femme fatale* take place in Rochester can serve as an overt intertextual reminder of Charlotte Brontë's *Jane Eyre*. Bertha Mason's act of vengeance which results in the burning down of Rochester's house that leaves her husband physically challenged resembles Rosalie's vindictive deed as both acts lead to the irreversible downfall of their male counterpart.

clothes to emphasize her physical attractiveness, even further supported by her "long mahogany hair [which] was lustrous" (*New Moon* 426) and her silky voice.

Meyer explicitly marks that Heidi is also clearly a *femme fatale* in her actions. She is "not only the fisherman, but also the bait" (*New Moon* 426) for the unfortunate, ignorant tourists that she leads to their own fatal death in the catacombs of Volterra. Through her self-determined, overtly erotic outward appearance and her apparent callousness towards humans she manipulates them with the help of her looks to follow her despite their own instincts and fear. However, the fatality that Heidi poses is only restricted to the world of the Volturi and does not inflict any damage on the protagonists.

The vampiric women of Tanya's coven in Denali also share a past that marks them as examples of demonic seductresses. As supernaturally attractive females they seduced men and later on fed on them. "In the end, it was their fondness for human men that turned the sisters against the slaughter. Now the men they loved … lived" (*Midnight Sun* 25). Edward teasingly calls Tanya a succubus (*Midnight Sun* 25) – a marked reference to the men-devouring demon from Christian mythology who feeds on its victim's vitality. Tanya still most of the time prefers human men to other male vampires because they are "much more populous for one thing, with the added advantage of being soft and warm. And always eager, definitely" (*Midnight Sun* 25). Meyer's intertextual markers of Tanya's preferences and her effortlessness in tempting human men are intended and display Tanya and her sisters as former *femmes fatales*.

Victoria takes up a different role. She is the greatest villain and antagonist for about two parts of the series. Already in her first appearance she is described as wild as her hair has "a startling shade of red" (*Twilight* 328), her walk is catlike, "constantly on the edge of shifting into a crouch" (*Twilight* 328) and "her posture […] distinctly feline" (*Twilight* 329). The references to her catlike physics relate well to her gift to have "some instinct for evasion" (*Eclipse* 77) that enables her to always escape at the proper moment: "Victoria was never going to give up […]. She would keep repeating the same pattern – feint and run, feint and run – until she found a hole through" (*Eclipse* 71). These characteristics also emphasize her animalistic appearance as being "wild, catlike, lethal" (*New Moon* 312) with her "vicious and feline figure" (*New Moon* 455) and her "oddly feline face" (*Eclipse* 112). Additionally enhancing her animalistic qualities, she is a "lioness waiting for an opening to spring" (*Eclipse* 480) and to revenge her mate in the end. Contrary to her wild outward appearance is her voice that has the sound of a child: "It was soft, it was high – a babyish, soprano tinkling.

The kind of voice that went with blond curls and pink bubble gum" (*Eclipse* 483). Victoria's voice that sounds overtly innocent and nearly angelic contrasts her lethal complexion and arms her with an alluring device to manipulate especially the men around her.

However, Victoria does not turn into a revengeful *femme fatale* until her mate, James, whom she was an accomplice to in his hunting games (*Twilight* 389) is murdered by Edward in order to rescue Bella from her ordeals. Bella imagines her as a thoroughly diabolical woman with her "eyes [...] black with thirst, bright with anticipation, and her lips curled back from her gleaming teeth in pleasure. Her red hair [...] brilliant as fire [...] chaotically around her wild face" (*New Moon* 221). The simile that compares "her flaming hair" (*New Moon* 488) to fire once more intensifies Victoria's exotic ferociousness and the danger she impersonates. Meyer repeatedly marks "Victoria's hair, blowing wild in the wind, the color of fire" (*New Moon* 335) as Bella sees it on the water. She allegorizes Victoria into a fateful, demonic force of nature tremendously threatening the lovers' relationship "like a hurricane moving toward the coast in a straight line – unavoidable, implacable, but predictable" (*Eclipse* 344). This is further stressed by the narrator's depiction of Victoria when Bella finally meets her for the second time, this time giving her the looks of a demon: "There was no wind here, but the fire around her face seemed to shimmer slightly, as if it were alive" (*Eclipse* 480). The diabolical qualities that Meyer attributes to Victoria are part of the archetypical characteristics that are associated with the demonic temptress, the *femme fatale*. Like the Lamia in Keats's homonymous poem who is "some demon's mistress, or the demon's self" (56) Victoria bears fiendish characteristics in her appearance.

Moreover, although Victoria cannot change her shape her feline posture that Meyer repeatedly draws on bears references to earlier depictions of *femmes fatales*. They could shape-shift from human to serpent and vice versa such as Lady Geraldine in Coleridge's *Christabel* who can evoke visions:

A snake's small eye blinks dull and shy,
And the lady's eyes they shrunk in her head,
Each shrunk up to a serpent's eye, [...]
One moment- and the sight was fled! (583-588)

Similarly, Keats' Lamia who is initially also portrayed as a snake with "her head was serpent, but ah, bitter-sweet! / She had a woman's mouth with all its pearls complete" (59-60) is only given a human shape by the help of Hermes.

Being a vampire generally arms Victoria with an overtly erotic female attractiveness that she fully unleashes on Riley with whom she has a sexual relationship[125] and whom she consciously sacrifices to death to approach her all-consuming aim of killing Bella and hurting Edward. She manipulates Riley into the belief that she really loves him in order to achieve her goal, thereby submerging fully into the role of the demonic seductress. The realization of his own fault in believing Victoria comes too late for him. She jeopardizes her lover's life for her aims and that also marks her as a descendant of Coleridge's female Life-in-Death from *The Rime of the Ancient Mariner* who plays dice for the mariner's life: "'The game is done! I've won! I've won' / Quoth she, and whistles thrice" (197-98).

Moreover, Victoria persuades Laurent to check if the Cullens are still around to protect Bella sending him on a fatal mission that eventually leads to his own destruction (*New Moon* 211). He "had been her first maneuver" (*Eclipse* 273). The sexually compelling effect that she obviously performs on others is deceptive. Love and sexual intercourse are only means to an end for Victoria, thus contrasting the protagonist's untainted relationship. Her noticeable erotic appearance which supports her ability to manipulate men is a characteristic that Victoria shares with her fatal predecessors. *Dracula*'s three temptresses are thoroughly lascivious so that they even tempt Van Helsing. They are "so full of life and voluptuous beauty that I shudder as though I have come to do murder" (*Dracula* 319). They can manipulate men just as easily as Victoria seems able to as Jonathan anticipates the vampire's bite "in a languorous ecstacy [sic] and waited – waited with beating heart" (*Dracula* 43).

In addition, Victoria displays a great fervidness in persecuting her goal so that it is possible to "feel the desire, the all-consuming passion that held her in its grip" (*Eclipse* 480). Her revenge also sets her up with a strong striving for power over others. The creation of her own army of newborn vampires explicitly shows her longing to rule over others. The power that she exerts over Riley is indestructible because although she is false and he is conscious of that (*Eclipse* 482) she has successfully manipulated him into believing her, promising specifically sexual pleasure. As such, he decides to "die for her lies" (*Eclipse* 482) and fight for her. Moreover, Victoria as a *femme fatale* not only manipulates others, she also violates social rules and breaches the vampires' law. The creation of an army of newborns is forbidden by the Volturi. Constituting a part of her vendetta her destructive non-compliance with the laws set up by the Volturi suits her lethal, fierce nature. As a *femme fatale* Victoria is malignant as much as she is fascinating, a consciously acting fatal woman who is actively

---

[125] Stephenie Meyer, *The Short Second Life of Bree Tanner – An Eclipse Novella* (London: Atom Books, 2010) 71.

seeking destruction and vengeance. In her fatality and cold-bloodedness she again resembles the female Life-in-Death from Coleridge's *The Rime of the Ancient Mariner* who dooms the mariner to an eternal life that she has won in a game of dice against Death. She represents a mixture of exceptional beauty and disease:

> Her lips were red, her looks were free,
> Her locks were yellow as gold:
> Her skin was as white as leprosy (190-92).

Bella, on the other hand, is not a *femme fatale*, not even after her transformation into a vampire. She is also described as "every bit as beautiful as Alice or Esme" (*Breaking Dawn* 372) and more than that "she's going to be dazzling. [...]You know what I mean. *Look* at her" (*Breaking Dawn* 353). In spite of everything she is not fatal or destructive to the ones around her. However, Meyer clearly marks that Bella surely has the capability to be lethal to others. While on her first hunt, Edward notes that the humans she almost hunted "probably wouldn't mind death if you were the one delivering it [...] they would think they were already dead and gone to heaven the moment they saw you" (*Breaking Dawn* 392). Nonetheless, Bella has the ability to stop herself in mid-hunt before she can actually become deadly to these humans (*Breaking Dawn* 386). Meyer constructs the only possible scenario for Bella to become lethal and fatal to others in the iterative dreams which she experiences before being transformed into a vampire – the ones in which she vehemently tries to protect a child from the Volturi.

In summary, Meyer applies the complete range of character traits that earlier female vampires and *femmes fatales* offer to her female characters. Female vampires in the *Twilight* series, eventually, either transport thoroughly friendship-seeking sentiments, although they are not as intimate with humans as their nineteenth-century predecessors Carmilla or Lamia, or they are destructive, tempting women like Lady Geraldine or Dracula's vampiric females. Intertextually, Meyer makes use of both depictions of female vampires of the nineteenth century, emphasizing their discrepancies between one another and approaching her pretexts through repeated references. To clearly show the connection between the female vampires that Meyer develops and their antecessors she repeatedly marks the most important intertextual characteristics of the vampiresses as already discussed.

Although Meyer does not implement direct quotations from her pretexts in regard to her vampiric females, apart from the straightforward reference to the succubus, and her characters are not aware of their own intertextual importance she does refer to their former qualities. However, these pretexts are not directly named which diminishes the potential of *communicativity* for the reader and the pretexts are also not structurally integrated in the given texts. Nonetheless, the attributes that Meyer chiefly draws attention to are the ones that mainly characterize female vampires in nineteenth-century literature. That sufficiently fulfils the criterion of *selectivity*. The dialogue that is achieved between pretext and subsequent text is significant. Although Meyer adopts specific features of the female vampire like the *femme fatale*, the outward appearance and the close bond that some predecessors have to humans, she openly denies them the form of true intimacy they formerly exerted.

5.1.4. Representations of Good and Evil

The representation of what is in general considered as good and what is evil is a concept that appears to be straightforward in nineteenth-century literature as vampires such as Dracula are clearly defined along the lines of evil while concepts as chastity or familial bonds are defined as good and pure. The idea of good is often opposed by something evil since it is usually the existence of the contrary concept that defines the other one. However, within a postmodern framework one often finds that what appears to be good turns out to be just as degenerated and tainted as that which at first seemed to be the prevailing evil. On the other hand, the evil which is pictured as threatening and malicious usually pinpoints and epitomizes the sometimes degraded nature of what is commonly considered good. Accordingly, there might appear to be no clear-cut boundaries between what is good and what is defined as evil. However, Meyer's conception of these two opposing ideas seems straightforward and more orientated on prior perceptions of good and evil.

Meyer's idea of abstinence appears to be woven into *Twilight*'s illustrations of good and evil. It is largely enacted through Edward and his vampiric family in their denial to nourish on human blood. Abstinence already functions as a significant idea for Stoker's *Dracula*. Jonathan and Mina's relationship never gets obviously intimate: "After lunch Harker and his wife went back to their own room, and as I passed a while ago I heard the click of the typewriter" (*Dracula* 199). The purity of their relationship and further specifically Mina's virtue "with all her goodness and purity and faith" (*Dracula* 268) is what contrasts her to the lascivious Lucy. Her "sweetness was turned to adamantine, heartless cruelty, and the purity to voluptuous wantonness" (*Dracula* 187) similar to the three voluptuous, highly sexualized vampiric females that live in Dracula's castle. Consequently, it is Mina's purity that eventually has to gain the victory over the vampires' vices. Abstinence in the *Twilight* series is primarily displayed through the Cullen's diet and their restraint to drink human blood. However, Edward takes the notion of abstinence to a new dimension. He abstains from biting Bella and transforming her into a vampire, although she repeatedly asks him to do it, just as he denies having sexual intercourse with her before they get married requesting of Bella to "*please* stop trying to take your clothes off" (*Eclipse* 399).

Although Bella only reluctantly consents to the agreement to marry Edward before she can become a vampire and can get truly intimate with her beloved one their relationship resembles the one that Jonathan and Mina Harker share. As a result, both couples function through their virtue and abstinence as juxtapositions to the sinful and voluptuous vampires who sustain themselves on human blood and have sexual intercourse. They are only able to fully consummate their relationship after Victoria and the Volturi do not immediately threaten them anymore as is the case for Bella and Edward. Mina and Jonathan have a baby which serves as a reminder of their hunting party as "his bundle of names links all our little band of men together" (*Dracula* 326) and Bella and Edward can finally enjoy their own happily ever after.

In the nineteenth century especially Gothic literature appeared to deal with varying concepts of good and evil, frequently portraying creatures such as monsters and vampires as the prevalent evil. They stand in opposition to apparently innocent humans who are preferentially damsels in distress that need to be protected for their chastity. This is fairly apparent in the dichotomy between Mina Harker and Lucy Westenra in Stoker's *Dracula* in which Westenra is turned into a voluptuous vampire and later on destroyed by the hand of her fiancé. Nineteenth-century vampires always ended up being portrayed as a form of evil that, if possible, needs to be annihilated. However, although Carmilla represents the obvious evil to the reader in Le Fanu's vampire tale she is also the only one who creates a truly intimate bond with the protagonist: a connection that the men in *Carmilla*, Laura's father, General Spielsdorf and Dr. Hesselius, remain unconscious of as they try to save Laura from approaching death brought about by Carmilla.

In Meyer's *Twilight* series there is also a constant interchange of ideas, concepts and characters that are considered along the lines of what is good and what is not. In the saga it is not vampires in general that are portrayed as evil but merely specific vampires and the institutionalization of these supernatural fantastic beings into feudal societies that crave more for power than for a harmonious co-existence. The Volturi and the nomadic vampire coven consisting of James, Victoria and Laurent are depicted as threatening and malignant.

Especially the differences between the nomads and the Cullens are highlighted as their "clothes were frayed, though, with wear, and they were barefoot" contrasting "the more polished, urbane stance" (*Twilight* 329) of the Cullens. As they are backpackers living without keeping a permanent residence Meyer depicts them as rather ferocious, animalistic and remote from society since they "exchanged a surprised look at the mention of the word 'home'" (*Twilight* 330).

On the other hand, the Volturi, the Italian group of extremely talented vampires, is displayed as "a very old, very powerful family [...]. They are the closest thing our world has to a royal family" (*New Moon* 17). Although they are, like most of the vampires in the series, pictured as beautiful, the Volturi are more than that described as being in their looks above every conception of human beauty – each one of them has "the exquisite face of a seraph" (*New Moon* 18), the highest rank of angels. They are marked as being the farthest away from any resemblance to humans. Aro is "as different from the vampires beside him as they were from me. His skin was translucently white, like onionskin, and it looked just as delicate [...] his eyes were red" (*New Moon* 411). The Volturi are the "essence" (*New Moon* 371) of vampires, the exact core to this type of supernatural creatures. At the same time they are "the substance of [...] nightmares, the dread behind your instincts" (*New Moon* 371-72) and the most threatening kind of vampires in the series.

Physically, they are similar to the two Romanian vampires, Stefan and Vladimir, who are eager to pick a fight with them, as they have "the same powdery look to their skin as the Volturi" (*Breaking Dawn* 581). Their voices, too, are reminders "of the ancient voices of Aro and Caius" (*Breaking Dawn* 580). Furthermore, they, too, used to be very powerful as "it was a sign of our power that everything came to us. Prey, diplomats, those seeking our favor" (*Breaking Dawn* 586). Since the two Romanians are strongly intertextually linked with Stoker's *Dracula* – Meyer explicitly marks them as "Dracula One and Dracula Two" (*Breaking Dawn* 586) – the Volturi are also connected to the vampire prototype as they share common characteristics.

Moreover, it is suggested that it is the Volturi's "love of power that binds them together" (*New Moon* 378) and that "they have assumed the position of enforcing our rules – which actually translates to punishing transgressors" (*New Moon* 379). This craving for power easily makes them corrupt as they "would manipulate their own sacrosanct law for gain" (*Breaking Dawn* 611). They are characterized as being hungry for power, an assumption that is already hinted at before the protagonist actually encounters them for the first time. This assumption of the Volturi as being not only complacent but forcefully situating themselves above others of their own kind and mainly caring about their self-interests is further emphasized by their outward appearance and behavior. All of them look ancient, their skin is translucently pale and Aro's hands are "papery" (*New Moon* 411) which denotes his old age. Their clothing which consists of "long robes [...] pitch-black, and brushed against the floor" (*New Moon* 411), immediately reminds the reader of Dracula's way of dressing which is depicted as "clad in black from head to foot" (*Dracula* 21). The Volturi's old age as well as Aro's gliding, otherworldly movements who only "drifted forward" (*New Moon* 411) instead of walking are further characteristics that they share with Dracula. He can move close to Jonathan without his slightest notice (*Dracula* 30-31). Furthermore, "of things and people, and especially of battles, he spoke as if he had been present at them all" (*Dracula* 33), thus hinting at his advanced age. References to the Volturi's age are frequently marked as Meyer repeatedly refers to their translucent, paper-thin skin, features and voice (*New Moon* 413, 414, 417, 421, *Breaking Dawn* 642), a description that evidently highlights their unearthly appearance which distinguishes them from others of their kind.

What mostly defines the Volturi as the series' most efficient depiction of malignant vampires is the constant threat that they pose to the lovers and the Cullen family. Although they are not substantially present for more than two scenes in the series they are a permanent menace to Bella and the Cullens which is further emphasized in their perpetual absence. Accordingly, Bella repeatedly emphasizes their threat in her urge to be transformed and also Aro's wedding present serves as a subtle reminder of this necessity. Bella and her vampiric family-to-be frequently make them an issue for discussion as they and their immediate actions and intentions remain obscure to the protagonist and the reader. The Volturi and the danger they pose are recurring in Bella's narration as the thought of them repeatedly penetrates the narrator's mind and enhances the sense of threat they pose: "Maybe the Volturi would come for me first – they'd kill me quicker, at least" (*Eclipse* 71). Even after her transformation into a vampire this fear is still apparent since she is "freed from old nightmares, from any dreams at all, [but still] it was impossible to forget the Volturi" (*Breaking Dawn* 491). Meyer's apparent sense for institutionalizing the Volturi further heightens their dangerousness as they "came in a rigid, formal formation [...] The faint brushing sound of their feet was so regular it was like music, a complicated beat that never faltered" (*Breaking Dawn* 631). The authority they radiate which is depicted as minatorial and menacing juxtaposes the familial structures of the Cullens as the Volturi are bound to each other by their desire for power while the Cullens are connected through the bonds of love, familial feelings and friendship.

The Volturi's relationship to humans is entirely malign. Similar to Dracula's demand that "your girls that you all love are mine already; and through them you and others shall yet be mine – my creatures, to do my bidding and to be my jackals when I want to feed" (*Dracula* 267) they regard humans as inferior beings. The Volturi see human beings as mere sources to nourish themselves as they "bring in their food from the outside" (*New Moon* 380) so that they do not have to leave Volterra until it is regarded as absolutely necessary. Dracula, too, values humans only as weak beings and mere food sources as they are "all in a row, like sheep in a butcher's" (*Dracula* 267). Dracula and the Volturi most thoroughly inhabit the notion of alienation that the vampire displays in Stoker's *Dracula*: it neither integrates in any way into society but rather enforces the presentation of the other nor is it consistently present throughout the narrative but rather referred to and talked about. The Volturi's disregard for the inferior humans that sustain them is similar to Dracula's view on the humans that he wants to rule over.

The obscured danger the Volturi threaten Bella and the Cullens with persists until the finale of the series. The threat Dracula poses to the diverse group of people that try to stop his attempt at infiltrating Victorian society and also Western civilization is as promiscuous and latent as the endangerment the Volturi pose. Almost like a shadow does Dracula stay in the characters' consciousness, always lurking there to assault them and their late nineteenth-century system of moral values as they arm themselves to hunt him: "Surely God will not permit the world to be the poorer by the loss of such a creature" (*Dracula* 270). Leaving the vampire without a voice of his own to articulate and justify his deeds and motivations after Jonathan Harker has left Dracula's castle makes him appear even more mysterious and volatile and debases him to a straightforward fully-fledged monster.

Victoria's position in the *Twilight* series is similar to Dracula's – both are being chased. Even more than the Volturi she is the permanent fear lurking in Bella's consciousness that leaves her incapable of action and disturbs her psychic balance: "Victoria. She'd come for me. I was dead. Not Charlie, too! I choked back the building scream" (*New Moon* 245-46). Meyer repeatedly marks Bella's fear of Victoria as the immanent threat which affects her physical health: "None of us were safe! Jacob the very least of all, if he was trying to put himself [...] between Victoria and me [...] I felt like I might be about to throw up again" (*New Moon* 278). The angst that Victoria arouses in the protagonist is only heightened through her demonic appearance with her blazing eyes and animalistic, catlike stature. Similarly, it is Dracula's outward appearance that already enhances his otherness as he begins "to crawl down the castle wall over that dreadful abyss, *face down*, with his cloak spreading out around him like great wings" (*Dracula* 39).

What iteratively produces fear in the *Twilight* series, more than the menacing fantastic creatures themselves, are the periods of absence that Meyer evokes in order to enforce the apparent sense of threat. The frequent latent reminders of the dangers that the Volturi and Victoria pose to Bella and Edward's relationship as well as their families and its result in achieving great tension in the protagonist's mind is what foremost creates the story's suspense of threat. Also *Dracula*'s villain is absent most of the time but still pushes the story forward with his absence and the consequences that his occasional deeds, eventually, trigger in the hunting group. Dracula is hardly left with any redeeming qualities. His declaration that he, too, has loved and his death which he endures "with a smile and in silence, […] a gallant gentleman" (*Dracula* 326) are the only instances in which he is depicted as approaching humanity. He easily displays the prevailing evil that penetrates society's norms and intrudes into established hierarchical structures. However, still pictured as the prototypical other and a threat to every societal moral value he remains the epitome of alienation and evil. In contrast, Meyer also endows the Volturi with a notion of good and although their manipulating character is greatly displayed, they "aren't supposed to be the villains […] They are the foundation of […] peace and civilization. Each member of the guard chooses to serve them" (*Breaking Dawn* 538). Nevertheless, Meyer does not show that within her tetralogy but clearly pictures the Volturi as a menacing feudal society.

As much as the Volturi and James' nomadic coven are regarded as forces threatening Bella and Edward's relationship and the familial structures set up by the Cullens, also the vampires that are initially displayed as good tend to have a number of characteristics that partly remove them from a conception of complete innocence and goodness. The faults that characters like Bella and Edward characterize are often self-serving but still simply imply that these faults are committed to protect their relationship and each other's life, for example as Bella wants Edward to stay out of the upcoming battle with Victoria and the newborns. Being aware that this will weaken his family in the fight "the guilt had my eyes glued to the table" (*Eclipse* 372) – a decision that also Alice makes when she tries to protect Jasper by telling a lie. Edward, too, makes such decisions as he willingly hurts Bella in order to let Jacob know that he succeeded in their rivalry for Bella's feelings by making her promise to marry him.

Meyer's conception of a conventional family whose representatives are part of the other in the series is presented as throughout good because they "stick together the way a family should" (*Twilight* 31) – being the most prominent example of a conventional efficiently-functioning family. Consequently, they most strikingly oppose the conception of the Volturi as a feudal court with a coterie perverted into a self-interested institutional form obsessed with power and control.

Another vital representation of the concept of good and evil is given in Meyer's construction of urban and rural surroundings. The heroine's first sentiments towards her new home in the provincial town of Forks are dismissive as it "was from this town and its gloomy, omnipresent shade that my mother escaped with me when I was only a few months old" (*Twilight* 3). Although her first impressions of Forks are that "it was too green – an alien planet" (*Twilight* 7) and "a damp green hole" (*Twilight* 24) her attitude easily changes as her feelings for Edward develop. Especially when she has to face James Bella wishes "for the green, protective forests of Forks... of home" (*Twilight* 386). Comparably, while Forks represents security, safety and the comforts of home to Bella and the Cullens, other places – namely Port Angeles, Phoenix, Seattle, Volterra, and Florida – stand for the dangers that can possibly damage the lovers' relationship and their families. Even Bella's visit to her mother in Florida raises questions concerning the constitution of their relationship. Similar to *The Man of Feeling*'s conception of cities as places of lurking mischief, risks and threats, the rural area as its counterpart is presented as the safe harbor for Bella and Edward's love, hence creating an intertextual reference that dwells on the dichotomy already achieved in Mackenzie's work.

Intertextually, the parallels between the representations of good and evil in Meyer's *Twilight* series and Stoker's *Dracula* are striking. Conceptions of evil find their most effective depiction in vampires who nourish themselves on human blood and are either voluptuous or try to manipulate others in order to assuage their own power-seeking inclinations. Marked intertextual references between the two works are especially apparent in the construction of the Volturi and the Romanians which both take up characteristics that are already evident in the construction of the vampires in *Dracula*. As the analogy between *Twilight*'s oldest vampires and Stoker's Count is drawn through Jacob's comparison of the Romanian vampires with *Dracula*'s villain this extra layer of meaning is, additionally, enhancing the intertextual value of the reference. Meyer endows the Volturi with another characteristic as they also represent the negative implications of an institutionalized force that corrupts and misuses its power. In contrast to Stoker who presents vampires in general as evil creatures that threaten

66

human society and familial structures, Meyer differentiates and makes it clear that some of her vampires are truly good while others at least have the choice to freely choose on which side they want to belong in the end.

Opposed to this display of the decay of moral values and norms it is the truly virtuous form of relationship that contrasts these representations of evil. The couples in *Twilight* and *Dracula* and the depiction of their own virtues are used in order to emphasize the juxtaposition between the two conflictive forces. The familial bonds which are created by mere necessity and affiliation rather than genetically-related blood bonds are formed and enhanced in order to oppose immanent threats in both works. Additionally, partially self-imposed abstinence connects the two couples and their self-chosen exceptionally-formed families in a number of ways.

5.1.5. The Vampire and Society

The vampire as a boundary-transgressing being inhabits a place in society, no matter if human or supernatural, that is remarkably unique. Other literary monsters and preternatural creations such as ghosts, zombies, and mummies have hardly exceeded their own position within society as the permanent other. On the contrary, the vampire with its ability to penetrate moral conceptions, hierarchical structures, as well as concepts of power and intimacy has achieved to position itself at various places within society over the past two centuries of its literary persistence. As such the vampire's status in diverse forms of society has the capacity, just as the penetrating creature itself to be strongly changeable although, as will be proven, some characteristics remain as constants.

The *Twilight* series' focus primarily lies on the vampiric family of the Cullens, whereas other vampires such as the Denali coven, the Volturi or James' nomadic coven are only minor characters in that they are indeed talked about and referred to but still most of the time physically absent from the story. Edward's family functions as the most significant example of Stephenie Meyer's depiction of an interrelation between the vampire and the numerous forms of society, in which it dwells or which it sometimes also opposes.

Besides the werewolf clan and the only marginally presented Quileute families, the Cullens display the most prominent efficiently-functioning conventionally-structured family in the *Twilight* series. They are contrasted by Bella's torn family which turns out to be more of a one-parent-family, the Volturi's corrupt institutional structures which primarily rely on hierarchical bonds, and the nomadics' loose constructions of family-affiliated patterns that are only desirable as long as they are useful to every participant of the party. The Cullen family, nevertheless, stands in a rather unilateral relation to the human society they repeatedly try to merge with. No matter how hard they try, their efforts are only finitely effectual as ordinary human "people always felt strangely ill at ease with the Cullens, almost afraid for some reason they couldn't explain for themselves" (*New Moon* 13). They are openly regarded as freaks at school – "The Cullens were freaks – everyone knew that already" (*Midnight Sun* 77) – during lunchtime Edward and Alice's classmates prefer to sit "on the other side of an invisible line. That line dissolved on sunny days when Edward and Alice always skipped school" (*New Moon* 13). Through their unworldly beauty which frightens humans as much as it fascinates them and their ability to seduce them – a characteristic that they share with preceding literary vampiric creatures like Keats' Lamia or Coleridge's Geraldine – they can merge with society but never fully be a real part of it. While especially young people shy away from the Cullens, adults like Charlie accept them without difficulties within their provincial society and Carlisle easily finds a job in the local hospital. So far they are in fact integrated into society. However, the Quileutes' response to the Cullens is initially hostile and only improves over time. Not only Edward but all the Cullens are outsiders to the human society that they try to approximate to – an actuality that is further emphasized as even animals shy away from them; "They all grew silent after we passed, their breath quickening in fear. The animals had a much wiser reaction to our scent than humans seemed to" (*Breaking Dawn* 382).

The Cullens vehemently try to fit into a community they know they can never fully belong to although Carlisle practices medicine at the local hospital and the others go to school just like normal adolescents do. However, still they are not fully accepted by other humans and they are avoided by the Quileutes who are not "going to the hospital since Dr. Cullen started working there" (*Twilight* 109). But also the Cullens' attempts to merge with the human small-town society of Forks are ambivalent. Edward is repeatedly irritated by the human thoughts that he, sometimes unwillingly, hears and develops numerous gory visions in which he imagines himself resorting to violence against the "generic, boring mortal" (*Midnight Sun* 92) Mike Newton. However, he cares for other humans after he falls in love with Bella when he asks for Carlisle's help in capturing the rapist who threatened his beloved. Other Cullens are even more eager to fit into their surroundings. Although Rosalie's dislike for Bella is apparant and goes as far as her suggestion to kill Bella in order to protect her family (*Midnight Sun* 82) and springs from her own jealousy for the protagonist, she also has an affinity for leading a life as ordinarily human as possible. She strongly desires this and the illusion of it is what she can most efficiently act out in Forks: "I *like* it here! There's so little sun, we get to be almost *normal*" (*Midnight Sun* 83).

However, the Cullens are not the first vampires who try to fit into their human surroundings. Nineteenth-century vampires have desired similar company, even if only to realize their own ambitions, and sometimes achieved it through somewhat different means. Lord Ruthven from Polidori's *The Vampyre* is a longtime participant of London's aristocratic society but he still "gazed upon the mirth around him, as if he could not participate therein" (*The Vampyre* 7). Ruthven does not radiate this air of threat towards humans and animals alike but rather attracts the females around him while the vampires in Meyer's series scare them. Only after spending a great amount of time with Ruthven does it appear to Aubrey, his companion on their journey through continental Europe, that Ruthven has an "appearance of something supernatural" (*The Vampyre* 10) about him. Still, the vampire's ability to merge with the human society around him does not seem to spring from his inherent wish to participate and be part of it but from a mere longing to fulfill his own desires and serve his wishes as he in the end "disappeared, and Aubrey's sister had glutted the thirst of a VAMPYRE!" (*The Vampyre* 24). His coalescence in human society is well-accomplished and effectual but only conducted to serve his own aims in completely seducing Aubrey's sister.

The nineteenth-century female vampire's interaction with human society is somewhat different. Carmilla's, Lamia's as well as Geraldine's contacts with humans are characterized through the intimacy they exhibit. Nevertheless, Carmilla's intimacy also springs from her desire for her partner's blood while Lamia and Geraldine's ambitions are to possess their partners. All of them expose a manipulative behavior in order to achieve their goals. However much they attain sympathy and intimacy with some humans, there are also others who look through them and see their supernatural nature and try to reveal their true nature. It is not surprising that the female vampire frequently is destroyed in the end.

The Cullens' contact with other humans is ambivalent in various ways. At times, their interaction with them is just as manipulating as is Carmilla's because "it was amazing the favors Edward could get the female administrators to do for him" (*New Moon* 11). They remain outsiders due to the humans' instincts that make people shy away from them as much as the protagonist's own alienation from human society throughout the series which enhances the vampires' peculiar status. Their outsider status is not only existent and obvious in their mainly futile attempts to fit into human society. They also exhibit the same status in their own supernatural world among the ones who incorporate the other as much as they do, thus emphasizing the Cullen's peculiar position as outsiders.

Among their fellow creatures of the fantastic the Cullens hold a position that is as unique as is their relation with humans or the status of the shape-shifting werewolves in the *Twilight* series. Being a rare exception in their dieting habits – along with the Denali coven – the Cullen family also appear to be a threat to other vampires as Rosalie notes that "we live so differently from the rest of our kind – you know there are those who would love an excuse to point fingers. We have to be more careful than anyone else" (*Midnight Sun* 82). Defined by their way of living and their formation of strong familial bonds that are unique among their species they stand out among others of their kind who feel that the Cullens in their otherness and especially through adaptation of family structures can be a danger to them. They pose a particularly potent threat to the Volturi's power in their alternative way of life and as they are "the biggest mature coven they've dealt with [...] closely bonded, and that's a factor" (*Breaking Dawn* 558). Consequently, they represent the epitome of otherness since they are as much outsiders to human society as they are special among their own vampiric species, naturally posing a threat to other vampires in their manifold otherness.

The Volturi's view of the Cullens and their allies is pejorative. Although they appear friendly and courteous at first glance, they are ill-natured and aggressively power-seeking in their aims and attitude towards them. "Their decision was already made, [as the Volturi were] just waiting" (*Breaking Dawn* 506) for Irina from the Denali coven in order to find a reason to attack the vampiric family in Forks as their "response to this kind of infraction was so automatic, it was already decided" (*Breaking Dawn* 507). The Cullens are thoroughly aware of the Volturi's abuse of their power and that they were yet waiting "for some pretext [...] but the plan was already in place for when it did come" (*Breaking Dawn* 561). Nevertheless, the Volturi's might and executive dominance over others of their kind is, at least among the nomads and other vampiric covens besides the Cullens, respected and trusted in as the idea that they might disobey their own rules made them uncomfortable (*Breaking Dawn* 611). The Italian vampires' intentions in either destroying the Cullens or persuading some of them to join the Volturi as "Aro didn't surround himself with second best" (*Breaking Dawn* 535) are apparently obvious. "They – Caius and Aro – come to destroy and acquire" and would be also eager "to find another reason to take offense" (*Breaking Dawn* 634).

The Volturi's ability to willingly manipulate the power that they usurped, initially in order to keep their race hidden from human knowledge, but misused to control others, resembles Dracula's attempts to usurp England and Western culture. Besides the striking similarities in outward appearance and movement, whose intertextual significance between Dracula and the Volturi has already been pointed out, both sides want to enlarge their numbers so as to increase their power and substantiate their own status. Aro was "a collector – and his most prized treasures were his living pieces. He coveted beauty, talent, and rarity in his immortal followers more than any jewel locked in his vaults" (*Breaking Dawn* 493). Comparably, Dracula claims that he will overpower his hunters in the end since he can possess the ones they love and time as well as mobility is on his side: "You think you have left me without a place to rest; but I have more. My revenge is just begun!" (*Dracula* 267). Although the Volturi and Dracula want to expand their powers, their attempts at expansion are not identical as the Volturi are singly interested in recruiting new members for their guard while Dracula wants to enslave Western civilization.

The vampires that Meyer creates in her *Twilight* series have manifold relations to the society in which they dwell. While the Cullens do not feed on humans and try to assimilate into human society although they only partially succeed in doing so, it is the Volturi's will to subordinate others. Whereas they forcefully aim at fortifying their power in the vampire world they regard humans as hardly more than a useful source for food – an attitude similar to that already displayed by the nomadic vampire James who believes Bella to be the Cullens' "snack" (*Twilight* 331). Neither the Volturi nor the nomads have any connection to human beings besides their reliance on the humans' blood. Their alienation from that part of society goes even farther than Dracula's as he can at least walk in the sun in London anonymously although his "white teeth [...] were pointed like an animal's" (*Dracula* 155), hence only being recognized by Jonathan but not by any other people.

Consequently, although not intertextually marked by references to Polidori's *The Vampyre,* Le Fanu's *Carmilla* or Keats's *Lamia*, the Cullens do become a part of society as much as they are able to. Meyer nevertheless repeatedly marks that there is no possibility for them to be fully integrated as their status as the other is irreversible. Similarly, also Carmilla and Lamia's attempts at assimilation into their surrounding environment fail due to their otherness and vampiric behavior. Only Dracula and Meyer's potentially most evil vampires are completely alien to human society displaying a threat that is universal and consistent in its dangerousness. As such, Meyer's vampires and their relation to the societies in which they live stand in line with traditional nineteenth-century representations of the other and the people surrounding them who are frequently fascinated by the other but most of the time only subconsciously aware of the dangers they position themselves into. Whereas the threat that vampires like the Cullens or creatures like Lamia display is only latent, the Volturi and James' nomadic coven are openly perilous. Meyer puts them alongside depictions of evil vampires such as Dracula and his three vampiric females who long for their victims' blood and the power they exert over them.

5.2. THE STAR-CROSSED LOVERS

As it is probably one of the most productive and meaningful themes in the *Twilight* series, the adaptation of the famous star-crossed lovers topos offers numerous intertextual references to examine and enrich the saga's meaning. Therefore, Meyer makes use of various pretexts from Shakespeare's tragic play *Romeo and Juliet*, Jane Austen's *Pride and Prejudice* to Emily Brontë's *Wuthering Heights* that all highlight differing components of the theme as it evolved and was further intensified throughout the centuries. As such the star-crossed lovers theme has created a topos that allegorizes all-consuming and irreversible love, insurmountable conflict as well as rigorous fatality in order to exhibit a great potential for intertextual markers in Meyer's work.

The star-crossed lovers in the *Twilight* series approach every aspect of this popular theme and partially shed new light on the topic. Conveying it into twenty-first-century literature gives the lovers a new outlook and opens up possibilities and dimensions which did not seem acceptable beforehand. As such, it will be necessary to look at some of the most significant cornerstones of the theme in order to determine how much Meyer truly relies on conventional characteristics of the topic through pretextual references and where the texts actually depart from that. The obstacles the lovers have to face in their fateful relationship as well as the tragic connection they share as their love is predestined and irreversible but also has the capacity to be fatally destructive can be considered as the most remarkable points of the theme. However, Meyer adds another, although not entirely new, layer of meaning. She broadens the topic through the bringing in of abstinence and sexuality and the monstrous fatefulness that can spring from it as she again turns to sources like Shelley's *Frankenstein* or Polanski's cinematic movie adaptation of *Rosemary's Baby*. Therefore, the incorporation of these criteria establishes vast room for intertextual references.

5.2.1. Obstacles to a Relationship

One of the most prominent constituents of the star-crossed lovers theme is the obstacles that oppose the lovers' choice of the respective partner. These interferences can be caused by a varied number of impediments that can range from differences in the lovers' ancestry, to the rivalry in love in which a third party intervenes into the lovers' lives or even simple miscommunication that can generate great misunderstandings leading to fatal decisions and actions. These barriers that hinder an unproblematic acting out of the lovers' feelings are not only numerous but are further inevitable in order to demonstrate the true nature of their passionate love and to enhance the fatality of a love that is predestined. These complications frequently enhance the suspense of the actions and events of the story.

Meyer applies a grand assortment of obstructions ranging from minor problems to insuperable barriers to the lovers, Edward and Bella, in her *Twilight* saga creating the possibility for intertextual references. When Bella meets Edward for the first time he appears to strongly dislike her as he reacts "with the strangest expression on his face – it was hostile, furious" (*Twilight* 20). Not only does he seem to dislike her, he also tries to avoid every physical contact as he "was leaning away [...], sitting on the extreme edge of his chair and averting his face like he smelled something bad" (*Twilight* 20). Bella believes that his "piercing, hate-filled eyes" (*Twilight* 24) transport hostile sentiments (*Twilight* 21). Although she is further irritated by his behavior which continuously changes from friendly and inquisitive to repellent, Bella's feelings for Edward are unalterable from the first day she sees him. This shows in her feeling that the next day was "worse because Edward Cullen wasn't in school at all" (*Twilight* 26). Nevertheless, she is strongly annoyed by his fickle attitude towards her which is characterized by alternate questioning and ignorance, a demeanor that further enhances his Byronic aura of mystery.

Comparatively, Edward's point of view of the incidents of their first acquaintance only marginally differs from Bella's human account. While she is confused by Edward's conflicting reactions to her, grounded in the belief of his repudiation, his thoughts and estimations of her behavior are similar to Bella's own evaluations. His first reactions to her, or precisely to her distinct scent, are apparently hostile: "I hated this frail woman-child beside me, hated her with all the fervor with which I clung to my former self, my love of my family [...] Hating her, hating how she made me feel" (*Midnight Sun* 14). These feelings are, nonetheless, only momentary as it merely takes him a second to realize that his "hate was unjust. I knew that what I really hated was myself" (*Midnight Sun* 16). Edward starts to feel jealous of Mike Newton and protective of Bella the next time that he sees her at school as he "didn't like the way his thoughts wrapped around her, the flicker of already established fantasies that clouded his mind while he watched her" (*Midnight Sun* 30). Although he tries to avoid thinking of Bella and worrying for her (*Midnight Sun* 31), his protective senses soon take over because "it was hard to believe that anyone so vulnerable could ever justify hatred" (*Midnight Sun* 35).

As their acquaintance with one another develops, new forms of misunderstanding emerge that puzzle both of them as they try to understand each other's actions and feelings. Edward's changing behavior that turns from protective and curious to hostile and disregardful is incomprehensible to Bella. Her attitude towards him remains similar to his as well, as she "gave no more notice that he existed than he showed toward me. I was miserable" (*Twilight* 60). Therefore, although both of them yearn to get to know each other more thoroughly, they both are restricted by the insecurities that trigger later misunderstandings and lead to fatal decisions. Edward's assumption that Bella will be disgusted by his vampiric nature – since this would be the normal human reaction to his kind – quickly becomes invalid. Still, his fears latently remain as he tells her, being afraid that she might be terrified of him after the fight against Victoria that "no one is going to hurt you. I won't touch you. I won't hurt you" (*Eclipse* 493). Moreover, he initially believes that Bella would be averse to becoming a vampire: "If I forced her into this empty half-life through my weakness and selfishness, surely she would hate me" (*Midnight Sun* 88). In return, Bella underestimates her own importance for Edward and the depth of his feelings as she repeatedly regards herself as not good enough for him (*New Moon* 62) and "nothing but a human, after all. Nothing special" (*New Moon* 277).

The misunderstandings that occur between the two lovers in the *Twilight* series go even further than simple misperceptions of the other one's feelings and actions. The complications that arise are in the beginning mainly due to their different ancestry. This not only implies difficulties because of their unique human-vampire-relationship but also Edward's moral conceptions and his views on matrimony and pre-marital sexual intercourse seem "very old-fashioned" (*Eclipse* 52) to Bella. As a result "Edward had drawn many careful lines for our physical relationship" (*New Moon* 15) in order not to accidentally hurt his beloved and because it is "the one area in which I'm just as spotless as you are" (*Eclipse* 403).

Edward's opinions on the fulfillment of a relationship are largely outdated and appear to spring from a nineteenth-century view on the world that is antenatal to him as Meyer marks his year of birth for 1901. Furthermore, Meyer inserts a reference that intertextually links Edward with the heroes of Jane Austen's novels as the hero of *Sense and Sensibility* was "named *Edward*. Angrily, I turned to *Mansfield Park*, but the hero of that piece was named *Edmund*, and that was just too close" (*Twilight* 128). Not only does the author endow her hero with an obviously popular name from the early nineteenth century but she also equips him with the moral characteristics of that time, thus enhancing the hero's intertextual potential as a modern-day adaptation of the Romantic hero.

The first part in the *Twilight* series takes up the structure of Jane Austen's *Pride and Prejudice* and uses it as an intertextual layer for the story in regard to the obstacles the lovers have to deal with. Nonetheless, most of the intertextual references to Austen's novel are covert, hidden in the characterization of the protagonists and the development of their love for one another. Both pairs of lovers have to face difficulties and overcome societal, economical and personal obstacles in order to accomplish their love. Similar to Edward, who is characterized as an outsider and only accepted within his family, Darcy is described as "proud, to be above his company, and above being pleased"[126]. Bingley is his sole true friend in the beginning. Darcy's pride and animosity for such societal events like balls leave him to be the only one in disregard of it and "the exclusion of all conversation" (*Pride and Prejudice* 24). He is as little accepted into the novel's rural society as Edward and his family are in Forks. Darcy's deprecatory comments on Elizabeth's plainness – just as Edward's initially hateful gazes at Bella – hurt her feelings and result in her bad opinion on him: "Everybody is disgusted with his pride. You will not find him more favourably spoken of by anyone" (*Pride and Prejudice* 68). Additionally, both men, who are likewise well-off, debase their future beloved ones as "not handsome enough" (*Pride and Prejudice* 13) or "ordinary human" (*Midnight Sun* 1) at the outset. Similarly, both are aware of the social, or in Edward's case natural, rules they violate by desiring the beloved one: "were it not for the inferiority of her connections, he should be in some danger" (*Pride and Prejudice* 47). As their love develops both men thoroughly observe their truelove (*Pride and Prejudice* 45, *Midnight Sun* 75) and begin to consider them as extraordinarily pretty.

Bella and Elizabeth, too, share characteristics that, furthermore, legitimate *Twilight*'s intertextual dependence on Austen's pretext. Elizabeth is worried and cares for her sister Jane regardless of her own health and as for Bella, "unlike most humans, her own needs were far down the list. She was selfless" (*Midnight Sun* 43). Bella and Elizabeth are both observing

---

[126] Jane Austen, *Pride and Prejudice* (Hertfordshire: Wordsworth Editions, 2007) 12. All quotes are taken from this edition, referred to as *Pride and Prejudice* in the text.

when it comes to other people. Consequently, Bella is also the first one to notice the change in Edward's eye color (*Twilight* 39) and the effect it has on his mood swings. As Elizabeth's disregard for Darcy makes her avoid him as much as possible, she observes others all the more. "With more quickness of observation [...] she was very little disposed to approve" (*Pride and Prejudice* 15) of the Bingley sisters who, as they represent the constraints of early-nineteenth-century society, oppose Bingley's wish to marry Elizabeth's sister. As both women get their feelings similarly hurt by their men through repudiation, Bella and Elizabeth have to overcome their initial repugnance for them and correct their first impressions in order to form a relationship with them. Besides the miscommunication that both parties have to resolve to be together, the obstacles which oppose their relationships are, although they are differing in both texts, numerous as well. Wickham, who villainizes Darcy, and the vampire James, who wants to kill Bella, threaten the lovers' relationship alike. Members of their own families disapprove of their relationships and try to interfere as for example Rosalie, whose aversion for Bella does not wear off until late in the series, or Mrs. de Bourgh and Bingley's sisters, who both depreciate a connection between Darcy and Elizabeth.

Meyer also applies a number of intertextual references to Austen's *Pride and Prejudice* that are fairly overt and enhance the story's reliance on the pretext. The narrator notes that Bella owns "a compilation of the works of Jane Austen [...] My favorites were *Pride and Prejudice* and *Sense and Sensibility*" (*Twilight* 128). According to Bella's mother Renée Bella looks like she "just stepped out of an Austen movie" (*Breaking Dawn* 41) on the day of her wedding, assuming that the theme for the marital ceremony is designed around Bella's wedding ring. Bella explains, however, that "the wedding wasn't actually centered around the ring, but around Edward himself" (*Breaking Dawn* 41).

The overt and covert references to Jane Austen's novels that Meyer establishes in the *Twilight* series are not only markers that display her use of *Pride and Prejudice* as a substantial structural layer for the first part of her tetralogy. She also applies a complete set of characteristics from Austen's novels to her series to construct the commencement of a star-crossed love, endow her hero with the belief in a moral system that dates back to the early nineteenth century and to deploy a number of obstacles and instances of miscommunication that her protagonists have to overcome. The difficulties that the hero and heroine face at the beginning of the series are constructed along the lines of Austen's novel complicating the protagonists' falling in love with each other.

In *New Moon* Meyer develops the obstacles that she already alludes to in the first part of her series even further. Especially the theme of the "ancient grudge"[127], the conflict due to the lovers' ancestry, takes center stage in the second part of the saga and generates new impulses for the novel through Meyer's treatment of the theme. Additionally, misunderstandings which were already evident in *Twilight* take on a new quality as they again enhance the story's intertextual significance and further lead to dramatic consequences for the characters involved.

More than in *Twilight* Meyer's deployment of overt intertextual references that she constructs from the very beginning of the novel shows her structural dependence on Shakespeare's *Romeo and Juliet*. She inserts a direct quotation from the tragedy into the paratext of her novel, thus introducing her reader to the pretextual significance that her work conveys. The recurring references that the author applies most notably at the beginning of the novel (*New Moon* 10) and when the story comes to its conclusion (*New Moon* 490) create an extensive framework of intertextual markers that highlight the pretext's most productive components for contextualization. As such, also the obstacles that Romeo and Juliet have to face and to overcome in order to consummate their relationship can be found in Meyer's *New Moon*.

While in Shakespeare's *Romeo and Juliet* the grudge occurs between two rivaling families, the main conflict in *New Moon* is transferred to the private sphere as it takes place between the human Bella and the vampire Edward. Nevertheless, the conflict between the vampires and the shape-shifting werewolves already emerges at this point of the saga. Bella's clumsiness and her will to become a vampire herself contradict Edward's opinion on his own damnation that triggers his decision to not take away Bella's soul. This private conflict is followed by a feud between the only two kinds of fantastic creatures in the series, the vampires and the werewolves, that takes place in the public sphere. Their antagonism for one another is depicted as instinctive and natural as for the werewolves to kill vampires is "what we are made for" (*New Moon* 273). They are strongly irritated by each other's scent – the one sensory perception that is crucial and instinctive to them and the most natural and intensive of their animalistic senses. The main conflict in *Romeo and Juliet* takes place in the public sphere as the two antagonistic families carry out their adversary sentiments. Their dispute is also natural and has no true cause as the two households "from ancient grudge break to new

---

[127] William Shakespeare, *Romeo and Juliet*, Brian Gibbons (ed.) (London: Methuen Drama, 1980) Prologue: 3. All quotes are taken from this edition, referred to as *Romeo and Juliet* in the text.

mutiny" (*Romeo and Juliet* Prologue: 4) and even the only governmental authority, Escalus, the Prince of Verona, acts ineffectually in his attempts to terminate the outbreaks of the families' feud. His appearance in the play is limited to only three scenes leaving most of the action without any institutional interference.

Similarly, the feeling of distrust and disgust that the Cullens and the Quileute shape-shifters feel for one another has no distinctively defined cause. Described as part of their instinct to regard the other one as their natural enemy, the conflict between the two incompatible parties is further enhanced as the repudiation for the other appears to be elemental to the composition of their characters. As the story develops Edward is able to make friends with Seth, which shows that "vampires and werewolves could get along just fine" (*Breaking Dawn* 10). However, the conflict still latently keeps on existing as the Quileutes' primary aim is "the safety of our families, of everyone here [...] Protect the tribe. Protect our families" (*Breaking Dawn* 183-84) and they are thus willing to kill Bella and her baby.

As the feud between the two families in Shakespeare's play starts to infect the lovers' private sphere and turns it into a private drama through Romeo's intervention in the fight between Tybalt and Mercutio, so does the quarrel between vampires and werewolves eventually intrude into the lovers' compromise to turn Bella into a vampire: "If any of them bite a human, the truce is over. *Bite*, not kill" (*New Moon* 493). In both stories the lovers' personal obstacles are intensified through the impact that the public conflict takes on their decisions. The personal conflict that exists between Romeo and Juliet springs from the lovers' rivaling families – their ancestry – that they easily overcome to consummate their relationship:

> Romeo would, were he not Romeo call'd,
> Retain that dear perfection which he owes
> Without that title (*Romeo and Juliet* II.2.45-47)

The union that they share is, however, only temporary as the public drama takes its toll on their relationship.

Meyer's construction of her lovers' private conflict fuels itself from constant intertextual references to Shakespeare's tragic play. As their differing ancestral roots and the danger that poses a threat to Bella's human life force Edward to tell her that he is "*tired* of pretending to be something I'm not, Bella. I am not human" (*New Moon* 62) Bella starts to see in Edward her "fickle Romeo" (*New Moon* 330). Edward, too, makes the conscious intertextual reference at the moment that he believes to be dead through the Volturi's hands when he personifies Juliet onto Bella by quoting Romeo's lines: "Death, that hath sucked the honey of thy breath, hath had no power yet upon thy beauty" (*New Moon* 399). Meyer dramatizes Edward and Bella's relationship through the deployment of various intertextual markers implying the star-crossed love that both couples experience and the utterly devastating obstacles that they have to deal with.

Besides the ancestral, social and personal difficulties that the protagonists have to overcome, the theme of miscommunication is essential to drive the plot to its tantalizing conclusion. This is evident in Meyer's novel as well as in Shakespeare's play as instances of miscommunication which only caused rather easily resolved misconceptions in Bella and Edward's first encounters lead to fatal actions and events in both works. Alice's wrong assumption of Bella's death and Rosalie's sudden phone call trigger Edward's suicide attempt and Bella's decision to, eventually, die, too: "I wasn't really planning on living much longer without seeing him. Or at all, if we were too late. It was comforting to know that I would have an easy out" (*New Moon* 380). Meyer already introduces this notion that is also a condition for the star-crossed lovers at the beginning of the novel when Edward and Bella discuss the options of a life without the other one initiated through a movie adaptation of *Romeo and Juliet* that they watch. Moreover, Bella's belief that Edward never truly loved her and left her for that reason is a form of miscommunication that not even his imagined voice, a recurring motif in *New Moon* and device for the inseparability of their all-consuming love, can convince her of.

Similarly, the fatality of messages that do not reach the appropriate addressee or are not being received at all is displayed throughout Shakespeare's play. The instance in which Romeo and his friends accidentally get the chance to read the list of invitees for the Capulet's ball causes the first act of miscommunication as they intrude into a social event they are not welcomed to. Romeo already foresees the fatal consequences of this act and his successive actions:

> Some consequences yet hanging in the stars
> Shall bitterly begin his fearful date
> With this night's revels, and expire the term
> Of a despised life clos'd in my breast
> By some vile forfeit of untimely death (*Romeo and Juliet* I.4.107-111)

As the play turns into a tragedy another instance of miscommunication initiates the play's catastrophe through Friar Laurence's failed message for Romeo. Just as Romeo believes his beloved to be dead and is determined to die just as soon, so is Edward in his decision to get killed as he is unwilling to accept any other contrary notice (*New Moon* 376). Meyer, once again, asserts a connection between the two works as Bella "remembered with painful clarity his words that day on the sofa, while we watched Romeo and Juliet kill themselves" (*New Moon* 376). The link that the author calls forth through the introduction of this shared theme is further stimulated by recurring, overt and covert, intertextual markers that again connect her work to Shakespeare's play.

A third barrier for Bella and Edward's relationship that Meyer heavily dwells on in the construction of her star-crossed lovers is the motif of rivalry that she invokes through the positioning of Jacob as a competitor for Bella's love. As an obstacle for the lovers it already pervades *New Moon* in which it is, however, only one impediment among others whereas in *Eclipse* it evolves into the major point of concern for Bella and Edward. Jacob, who helps Bella to deal with Edward's inevitable absence, takes on the position of the suitor. *Romeo and Juliet*'s Paris is considered brave, without any flaws (*Romeo and Juliet* I.3.76) and remarkably handsome as one can "read o'er the volume of young Paris' face / And find delight writ there with beauty's pen" (*Romeo and Juliet* I.3.81-82). He is described as "a gentleman of noble parentage, / Of fair demesnes, youthful and nobly lign'd" (*Romeo and Juliet* III.5.179-80). Similarly, Jacob is strong, connected to Bella through a persistent bond of friendship and depicted as "sort of beautiful" (*New Moon* 168). Moreover, Paris and Jacob are both favored by their adored one's parents. Capulet encourages Paris to court Juliet as his "will to her consent is but a part" (*Romeo and Juliet* I.2.17-19). As such, he also decides that Juliet "shall be married to this noble earl" (*Romeo and Juliet* III.4.21) without her own consent.

Likewise, Charlie supports Jacob in his attempts to convince Bella of his feelings for her as he is "practically family" (*Eclipse* 11) and preferred by Charlie. At the same time his dislike for Edward becomes obvious as he was "doing his best to illustrate the theme of 'unwelcome' with every word and posture" (*Eclipse* 4-5) whenever Edward is at Bella's home. It also does not bother him that Jacob kisses his daughter against her will as he "ought to sound a bit less amused and a bit more concerned" (*Eclipse* 298).

Many of the intertextual references that Meyer draws to illustrate the rivalry between Edward and Jacob and to position them similarly to Romeo and Paris due to the means of interfigurality are overt. Especially the denomination of a chapter as "Paris" and the use of multiple markers that construct Jacob as the suitor of Bella as well as a descendant of Shakespeare's Paris create a strong intertextual significance in Meyer's work. When Bella dreams about *Romeo and Juliet* – "a set on a stage. A balcony at night, a painted moon hanging in the sky. I watched the girl in the nightdress lean on the railing and talk to herself" (*New Moon* 325) – she immediately links her own situation to Juliet's wondering what she would have done if Romeo had left. As Meyer lets her protagonist meditate on Paris she endows her own Paris with qualities that are inexistent in his predecessor: "What if Paris had been Juliet's friend? Her very best friend? [...] What if he really loved her, and wanted her to be happy?" (*New Moon* 325-26). Through the positioning of Jacob as Bella's best friend and someone she cannot live without Meyer inaugurates the possibility of an alternate ending for both Juliet and Bella. Nevertheless, for Bella it would be "downright miserable to give up my hallucinations and try to be a grown-up. But maybe I should do it. And maybe I could. If I had Jacob" (*New Moon* 327). The alternative that Meyer evokes enforces the obstacle of rivalry for the lovers as it makes Jacob into a more potential and stronger rival for Bella's love than Paris ever had the opportunity to be for Juliet. Whereas Jacob who has "become essential to my survival" (*New Moon* 329) actually resurrects feelings of love in Bella, Paris is neither capable nor close enough to the woman he desires to achieve that.

The threat that Jacob poses to the lovers' relationship is especially evident in *Eclipse* since Meyer models that third part of her tetralogy on Brontë's *Wuthering Heights*. Once more intertextual references are continuously apportioned throughout the entire novel and a copy of the book itself functions as a prop in the story (*Eclipse* 7, 16, 235). However, Meyer does not repeatedly insert references to Brontë's novel in order to link Jacob with Edgar but to address the difficulty of choice and the rivalry between Edward and his opponent. Whereas the private conflict between the two star-crossed lovers is in general solved at this point of the story, the public feud between the vampires and werewolves gets the upper hand, as exemplified in the dispute between Edward and Jacob.

Meyer, once again, makes use of the concept of interfigurality as she draws overt parallels between the two male protagonists. Edward is "discovering that I can sympathize with Heathcliff in ways I didn't think possible before" (*Eclipse* 235), playing on Heathcliff's vampiric qualities[128] as well as their common status as Byronic heroes and their take on rage and revenge. Covertly, Meyer addresses this rage when Edward spots Bella's charm bracelet: "For a fleeting moment, I was afraid. Just the slightest twist of his fingers could crush it into splinters" (*Eclipse* 365). Similarly to Heathcliff, Edward leaves the one he loves because of diverse instances of misunderstanding and miscommunication as he is convinced that Bella

---

[128] Lakshmi Krishnan extensively discusses Heathcliff's vampiric qualities in an essay concluding that Heathcliff can, in fact, be regarded as a vampire. Cf. Lakshmi Krishnan, "'Why am I so changed?': Vampiric Selves and Gothic Doubleness in 'Wuthering Heights'," *Journal of Dracula Studies*, Nr. 9, 2007, 1 Nov. 2010 <http://www.blooferland.com/drc/images/6/68/09Krishnan.rtf>.

will be better off without him. In both novels the women that are left behind rely on other men to compensate for the beloved one they lost. However, whereas Jacob and Bella are bound by deep friendship for one another, Cathy marries Edgar primarily because "he will be rich, and I shall like to be the greatest woman of the neighbourhood" (*Wuthering Heights* 78). There are no deep feelings in Cathy towards Edgar while Bella truly feels love for Jacob. Cathy even despises her husband: "I don't want you, Edgar. I'm past wanting you. Return to your books. I'm glad you possess a consolation, for all you had in me is gone" (*Wuthering Heights* 118). However, both women have to make a choice in which Bella assumes similarities between herself and Cathy: "I was like Cathy, like *Wuthering Heights*, only my options were so much better than hers, neither one evil, neither one weak" (*Eclipse* 459). The decision that Bella makes is predetermined through the all-consuming love she feels for Edward. Whereas Cathy's decision in favor of Edgar is determined by social and financial constraints as well as by the class she's born in it is precisely these obstacles caused by different ancestry that Bella longs to overcome. Nonetheless, Jacob would have been "the natural path your life would have taken [...] If the world was the way it was supposed to be, if there were no monsters and no magic" (*Eclipse* 530-31).

The intertextual links that Meyer provokes between her characters and the protagonists of *Pride and Prejudice*, *Romeo and Juliet*, and *Wuthering Heights* evoke a strong intertextual significance. Not only does Meyer use these pretexts as layers to construct three volumes of her tetralogy in a similar way, through the implementation of multitudinous overt intertextual references, direct quotations as well as the appearance of copies of her pretexts as props within her work, she is able to illustrate the obstacles that her star-crossed lovers have to overcome. Meyer also endows her protagonists with the knowledge of their own interfigurality as they compare themselves to the other one as well as their own actions and feelings to their pretextual counterparts in *Romeo and Juliet* and *Wuthering Heights*. The degree of intertextuality that the author achieves is tremendous as references are easily made apparent to the reader, too.

Moreover, the particular obstacles that Bella and Edward have to face in order to consummate their love are deeply rooted in the theme of the lovers who are driven by fate as they are also apparent in earlier treatments of the theme. Meyer deploys its components – miscommunication, conflict due to ancestry, and rivalry – differently than her predecessors did as her star-crossed lovers are not overpowered by the obstacles they need to endure. They are able to succeed in overcoming the difficulties that other pretextual lovers were forced to surrender to, thus only being left with the possibility for a complete reunion in death. Although Bella, too, has to die to obtain a truly equal relationship with her beloved, Meyer creates through her insertion of an entirely fantastic context the possibility of avoiding final death and to replace it by means of eternal existence. As such, Meyer is able to construct for her protagonists the opportunity to vanquish their difficulties which her predecessors did not.

5.2.2. Lovers driven by Fate

Apart from the numerous obstacles that star-crossed lovers like Edward and Bella have to face in order to fully consummate their relationship, their love might be further categorized as an all-consuming, unchangeable and irreversible force. This form of love often turns out to be fatal to the lovers as prominent pairs of star-crossed lovers such as Romeo and Juliet or Heathcliff and Cathy show. Meyer acknowledges that "these violent delights have violent ends" (*New Moon* Paratext) through the quotation she inserts into the paratext of the second volume of her tetralogy. The already implied power and force that this kind of love conveys is extraordinarily strong.

Closely linked to the theme of the star-crossed lovers has always been the concept of love at first sight. *Romeo and Juliet* greatly displays this idea as Romeo immediately falls for Juliet when she enters the Capulet's ball with her parents and her cousin Tybalt: "Did my heart love till now? Forswear it, sight. / For I ne'er saw true beauty till this night" (*Romeo and Juliet* I.5.51-52). Romeo's first words to his beloved start a sonnet that both lovers share and that eventually ends in a kiss, thus setting a new, private tone for the lovers' conversation that sets them apart from the rest of the ball. They effectively exclude themselves through the implementation of the sonnet, and the motifs of hands, pilgrimage and sin exemplify their feelings. As they begin their second sonnet they are interrupted by Juliet's nurse whose disruptions foreshadow later complications and obstacles that the lovers have to face as well as the ultimate failure of achievements.

Although Meyer creates various intertextual connections to the lovers in Shakespeare's play in the depiction of her own star-crossed lovers, Edward and Bella do not experience a similar first moment of love at first sight. When Edward sees Bella for the first time in the thoughts of his fellow human students he regards her as "just another ordinary human girl" (*Midnight Sun* 1). His first reaction to seeing her with his own eyes is that he "looked away, bored" (*Midnight Sun* 4) by the unexceptional actions in the school cafeteria. Nevertheless, his instincts tell him to protect her, even from something as trivial as Jessica's unkind sentiments: "I felt a strange impulse, one I did not clearly understand. [...] I felt the strangest urge to step in between them, to shield this Bella Swan from the darker workings of Jessica's mind. What an odd thing to feel" (*Midnight Sun* 8). As his protective instinct awakes even the appeal of her blood that "hit me like a wrecking ball, like a battering ram" (*Midnight Sun* 9) cannot make him hate her or seek her life.

Their first encounter and the irresistible allurement that Bella's scent has to Edward so that he repeatedly "saw the same face" (*Midnight Sun* 24) whenever he closed his eyes initiates a change in him towards his own, previously lost, humanity that makes him fall in love with Bella more and more. She, too, feels attracted to him from the very first day as she misses him the next day when he does not appear in school (*Twilight* 26). Both experience their first physical encounter similarly as they conjointly associate it with electricity. For Edward it was like "the heat of her skin burned into mine. It was like an electric pulse" (*Midnight Sun* 38) that hit him unexpectedly. Comparably, for Bella "it stung my hand as if an electric current had passed through us" (*Twilight* 38).

Meyer's construction of Bella and Edward's first encounters is apparently different from Romeo and Juliet's instant act of irrevocably falling in love with one another. However, Meyer's lovers are also able to achieve a similar moment when they unintentionally touch for the first time. The electric current that both of them feel initiates the first moment which they commonly share. The physicality of this first touch contrasts the concept of abstinence that Meyer evokes to characterize the greatest part of the lovers' relationship. Whereas a sexual consummation of their love is delayed until after marriage, the foundations of their love are defined by physicality. Besides their first touch, especially Bella's heart as it "lurched frantically" (*Twilight* 305) or entirely "stopped beating" (*Twilight* 168) for seconds as a reaction to Edward's presence, physical contact, and kisses displays notions of physicality. Heightened by the alluring scent that draws Edward to Bella and Edward's "crooked smile" (*Twilight* 38) that mesmerizes Bella, Meyer innovates the concept of the love at first sight through a love that is also generated by first touch and scent.

Bella's compelling scent and Edward's inability to read her thoughts as well as her lack of instinctual fear of the unknown and other are not without a cause. The emergence of the love that binds Bella and Edward to one another is driven by fate and irrational as it is biologically determined. Aro refers to Bella as Edward's "la tua cantante" (*New Moon* 415), someone whose blood sings to him, a coincidence that also happens to Emmett twice. Edward's brother, however, is guided by his natural impulse to instantly feed on the girls' blood. In contrast, the origination of the love between Heathcliff and Cathy at first seems obscure as Nelly Dean notes that "on coming back a few days afterwards (for I did not consider my banishment perpetual) [...] Miss Cathy and he were now very thick; but Hindley hated him" (*Wuthering Heights* 46). As their relationship develops it becomes evident that their love is also natural as they are each other's soul. Eventually, for all of these three pairs of star-crossed lovers the moment of discovering this love comes likewise unexpectedly as the reasons for it tend to be biologically determined and natural.

Another feature of the star-crossed love that Meyer, too, repeatedly alludes to is its ability to be all-consuming and larger than life as it holds the capability to be tremendously devastating even to the lovers themselves. From the moment their love for one another develops it is also characterized by an absolute inability to endure life without the beloved one. Edward's decision to die in case of Bella's death at James' hands, as "part of my mind was making contingency plans" (*New Moon* 17) exemplifies the necessity of a shared life and death. Embedded into the context of a *Romeo and Juliet* movie adaptation Edward acknowledges that "I wasn't going to live without you" (*New Moon* 17). Similarly, Bella is determined to forfeit her life in case of her beloved one's death: "I did not intend to survive [...] Maybe I didn't *want* to survive, no matter what happened" (*New Moon* 382). Bella, too, notes that "I was glad something bloodthirsty waited in the wings. For in failing at this, I forfeited any desire to live" (*New Moon* 2). It is precisely this fateful notion of the star-crossed love theme that Meyer uses to frame the second novel of her series as she positions a reference to it into her preface enhancing the story's suspense.

Comparably to Edward, who instantly makes up his mind to go to the Volturi as he hears of Bella's suicide, Romeo decides to die the moment Balthasar brings him the news of Juliet's death:

Juliet, I will lie with thee tonight.
Let's see for means. O mischief thou art swift
To enter in the thoughts of desperate men (*Romeo and Juliet* V.1.34-36)

Romeo and Edward's inability to live on without their truelove is mirrored by Bella and Juliet's desperate fixation to die, too, as Juliet speedily takes the dagger to stab herself. Likewise, Heathcliff and Cathy are not able to live without the other. Heathcliff claims that "I could as soon forget you as my existence" (*Wuthering Heights* 142) when Cathy lies dying and that "misery and degradation, and death, and nothing that God or Satan could inflict would have parted us" (*Wuthering Heights* 144). When Cathy eventually dies, the only thing that prevents Heathcliff from dying at her grave is Cathy's ghost that he imagines to haunt and console him for the rest of his life: "A sudden sense of relief flowed from my heart through every limb. [...] when I walked on the moors I should meet her coming in. When I went from home I hastened to return: she *must* be somewhere at the Heights, I was certain!" (*Wuthering Heights* 242).

The notion of the star-crossed lovers theme which all the couples share is an inability to exist without the beloved one as it is a necessity. Furthermore, for all of them the extinction of one means death for the other, as well. The lovers are also frequently depicted as two parts of one thing and if one of them leaves, something essential is missing in the other one and vice versa. Cathy and Heathcliff repeatedly display the all-consuming passion that they feel for one another through the bestowal of their souls with their lovers. Both of them state that they are unable to exist without the other one as Heathcliff declares: "I *cannot* live without my life! I *cannot* live without my soul!" (*Wuthering Heights* 148). As a result a crucial part of themselves would die with the beloved as for Cathy "he's more myself than I am. Whatever our souls are made of, his and mine are the same" (*Wuthering Heights* 80).

Meyer adopts this notion of the inseparability of the lovers as she repeatedly dwells on it in the construction of her symbols and motifs. The hole in Bella's chest that is "excising my most vital organs and leaving ragged, unhealed gashes around the edges that continued to throb and bleed despite the passage of time" (*New Moon* 105) symbolizes her missing heart that left when Edward did. Once more, Meyer draws on notions of physicality to emphasize the importance of the lovers' relationship. Edward leaves her broken and torn as she is incapable to lead a normal and happy life without him. Indeed, his disappearance was to her "like someone had died – like *I* had died" (*New Moon* 350) as she was left "broken beyond repair" (*New Moon* 192). Instead of the lover's soul that the beloved one owns, Meyer asserts that it is the heart that stays with the truelove as also Edward acknowledges that "it was like my heart was gone – like I was hollow. Like I'd left everything that was inside me here with you" (*New Moon* 454).

Edward's hallucinated voice is another symbol that depicts the inseparability of the star-crossed lovers as it displays Bella's all-consuming love for Edward and her inability to live through the days without him. The silence that Meyer evokes after Edward's abandonment of Bella, which covers a period of four months and leaves the reader without any information on the protagonist's feelings and actions, displays a mental perishing on

Bella's part. Her inability to communicate her thoughts and feelings in the beginning of Edward's absence shows the fundamentality of the love they share. Edward's hallucinated voice develops into a necessity for Bella that is indispensable to her life. When she imagines his voice for the first time "everything was very clear. Like my head had suddenly surfaced out of some dark pool. I was more aware of everything" (*New Moon* 99). Although she is aware of the pain that hearing his voice triggers in her, Bella is repeatedly willing to put herself in danger in order to listen to the remains of her love as "those precious moments when I could hear him again were an irresistible lure" (*New Moon* 141). She even endures physical pain to enjoy her own hallucinations: "My velvet-voiced delusion had yelled at me for almost five minutes before I'd hit the brake too abruptly and launched myself into the tree" (*New Moon* 170). As she "would do anything for that voice" (*New Moon* 270) she even risks her life by jumping off the cliff. Edward's imagined voice eventually almost gets Bella killed during his physical absence although it is also what keeps her going during that time.

Similarly, it is Cathy's imaginary presence that keeps Heathcliff alive during the eighteen years after her death. While he is never able to see Cathy's ghost even though he again and again tries to see her, her disembodied presence makes him endure the time without her. His attempts to see her "a hundred times a night" (*Wuthering Heights* 242) are vain but similarly to Bella who "was addicted to the sound of my delusions. It made things worse if I went too long without them" (*New Moon* 310) he is entirely unable to stop trying. Bella as well as Heathcliff are incapable of living without the illusion that some part of their beloved one is still with them. Cathy's ghost and Edward's voice are delusive and lead Bella and Heathcliff into doing things that are either destructive or dangerous. Their inability to take on a life without the beloved one characterizes their star-crossed love as it is irreversible and leaves feelings for the other one unchangeable. Furthermore, it makes it impossible for them to fall in love with somebody else as "I would never want anything but him, no matter how long I lived" (*New Moon* 398).

Along with the incapability to live without one's respective partner goes a deeply-rooted knowledge of togetherness. This certainty of knowing that one deserves the other and is destined to be with that person is most evident in Bella's epiphany which she experiences after Edward's return: "The bond forged between us was not one that could be broken by absence, distance, or time. [...] he was as irreversibly altered as I was. As I would always belong to him, so would he always be mine" (*New Moon* 465). It is Jane Austen's *Mansfield Park* that displays this notion of deserving the other most clearly as Fanny and Edmund deserve one another because "Fanny was indeed the daughter that he wanted [...] and the general goodness of his intentions by her, deserved it"[129]. Although Meyer only deploys one overt intertextual reference to Austen's *Mansfield Park*, her references to other novels by the author establish a framework of intertextual markers that refer to Austen's overall work.

Meyer takes the notion of the inseparability of the lovers even further as she deploys the motifs of drugs, addiction, celestial bodies as well as states of light and darkness as symbols for the relationships of the protagonists. Moreover, these symbols display the power of the star-crossed love to change the ones it strikes, as it alters them irrevocably. As such they unfold their meaning most effectively when they display fateful decisions that influence the characters' lives. Bella decides that it does not matter who Edward is as she stands in the middle of the forest where "the rain made it dim as twilight" (*Twilight* 121). Symbolizing the impact of Bella's decision as it affects the turn of her life, Edward notes that twilight signifies "the end of the day, the return of the night" (*Twilight* 204) and always the possibility of a change just as the advancement of something new – a notion that is once more taken up through Edward (*Twilight* 430). Similarly, the new moon in Meyer's novel of the same title allegorizes a change that is tremendous in its effect on the heroine. Once again Bella finds herself in the middle of the forest in complete darkness this time being left by Edward. "Tonight the sky was utterly black. Perhaps there was no moon tonight – a lunar eclipse, a new moon. A new moon. I shivered, though I wasn't cold" (*New Moon* 65-66). At this point the new moon functions as a symbol for Bella's life after Edward leaves Forks. Her existence without her beloved one resembles an endless, dark night as the separation from him leaves her without any options to lead a happy life.

Whereas twilight and the new moon denote change and the impact of decisions in Meyer's series, other celestial bodies emblematize the depth of love that the star-crossed lovers share. Jacob addresses the totality and hopelessness of such a love in his abdication of the rivalry for Bella's love when he acknowledges "the clouds I can handle. But I can't fight with an eclipse" (*Eclipse* 531). Edward's absence appears thoroughly destructive to Bella's life as it takes away its every sense and puts her in a condition that resembles a vegetative state because she loses her entire vitality. An eclipse – the obscuring of one celestial body through another one – leaves the heroine in a state of complete darkness from which she is unable to re-surface until her beloved one returns. Another image of light and darkness is

---

[129] Jane Austen, *Mansfield Park* (Hertfordshire: Wordsworth Editions, 2007) 379.

picked up by Edward in his description of his existence prior to his and Bella's first encounter:

> My life was like a moonless night. Very dark, but there were stars – points of light and reason... And then you shot across my sky like a meteor. Suddenly everything was on fire; there was brilliancy, there was beauty. When you were gone, when the meteor had fallen over the horizon, everything went black. Nothing had changed, but my eyes were blinded by the light. I couldn't see the stars anymore. And there was no more reason for anything. (*New Moon* 454)

Just like Bella's life, his is fundamentally changed through the encounter with Bella. His life after the breakup appears meaningless and devastating in the same manner and he is also incapable of returning to a status in which he could at least appreciate again what he found delight in before he met Bella. The eclipse and the meteor figuratively symbolize the irreversibly life-changing aspect of the star-crossed lovers theme as it furthermore denotes the absurdity and unacceptability of a life beyond that love.

Another symbol that Meyer endows her series with is the moon as a satellite orbiting around another planet. This symbol again depicts the dependence of the one upon the other but it moreover displays Bella's own dependence on Edward as she is like "a lost moon – my planet destroyed in some cataclysmic, disaster-movie scenario of desolation – that continued, nevertheless, to circle in a tight little orbit around the empty space left behind" (*New Moon* 177). Even after Edward's return she relies on him for everything as Renée notes: "When he moves, even a little bit, you adjust your position at the same time. Like magnets ... or gravity. You're like a ... satellite, or something" (*Eclipse* 61).

The sun as another celestial body is applied by Meyer as a symbol for hope and positive change. Bella regards Jacob as "an earthbound sun, whenever someone was within his gravitational pull, Jacob warmed them. It was natural, a part of who he was" (*New Moon* 128). More than once she refers to him as her own "personal sun" (*New Moon* 174, *Eclipse* 531) – a characteristic that Meyer also deploys in her characterization of Jacob as his smile looks "the way the sunrise set the clouds on fire" (*New Moon* 192). He is further described as "sunny and warm" (*Eclipse* 158) – that made it at least possible for her to endure the darkness Edward left behind a little bit better. When Jacob tries to ignore Bella after he has found out about his shape-shifting skills, it seems to Bella "like my sun had imploded" (*New Moon* 231). Nevertheless, he is never more than her "replacement sun, the warmth that made my empty life livable" (*Eclipse* 438). On the contrary, Edward notes that the love he feels for Bella gives him a reason to live as his "life was an unending, unchanging midnight. [...] So how was it possible that the sun was rising now, in the middle of my midnight?" (*Midnight*

Sun 109). What he experiences is an unconditional change in him that also affects his personality to the extent that life no longer will be dull and dreary to him. This change is "a rare and permanent thing" (*Midnight Sun* 109) and bears the same effect as Bella's decision in the forest.

Meyer's recurring use of celestial bodies as symbols is intertextual as Shakespeare, too, uses celestial bodies like the sun and the stars in *Romeo and Juliet* in his imagery of light and dark to display the lovers' feelings for one another. On seeing Juliet for the first time, Romeo exclaims that "she doth teach the torches to burn bright! / It seems she hangs upon the cheek of night" (*Romeo and Juliet* I.5.43-44). Juliet's beauty is beyond the blaze of a torch as she enriches the night through her light and her eyes are "two of the fairest stars in all the heaven" (*Romeo and Juliet* II.2.15). Furthermore, Romeo says that "Juliet is the sun" (*Romeo and Juliet* II.2.3), thus making her essential for all life, without whose existence also Romeo could not exist. Juliet, too, compares Romeo to celestial bodies like the stars when she claims:

> when I shall die
> Take him and cut him out in little stars,
> And he will make the face of heaven so fine
> That all the world will be in love with night,
> And pay no worship to the garish sun. (*Romeo and Juliet* III.2.21-25)

Her demand to transform her lover into little stars so that everyone can see him for eternity addresses the timelessness of the love they share for each other and positions their love above the ordinary as it is unearthly.

Meyer applies further metaphorical imagery in her endowment of the series with a number of motifs concerning drugs and addiction that similarly illustrates the inseparability of the lovers and their inability to exist without the beloved. Edward describes the lure that Bella's scent poses to him in terms of this: "you are *exactly* my brand of heroin" (*Twilight* 235). Comparably, Bella develops a "hopeless addiction to him" (*Twilight* 255), illustrating that both of them are unable to live without the other one – a conclusion that also Jacob makes when he notes: "He's like a drug for you, Bella [...] you can't live without him now. It's too late. But I would have been healthier for you. Not a drug" (*Eclipse* 531). As such, it becomes vital to her to cling to Edward's hallucinated voice when he leaves her as she becomes addicted to the sound of his imagined voice. This addictive behavior in relation to Edward does not even change after her transformation into a vampire as still his "lips were like a shot of some addictive chemical straight into my nervous system. I was instantly craving more" (*Breaking Dawn* 467). The feelings she generates for Jacob are another measure of keeping herself alive that turns into an addictive behavior: "I wanted to see Jacob. Maybe I was developing a new kind of sickness, another addiction" (*New Moon* 143). Being essential to her survival she "needed Jacob now, needed him like a drug" (*New Moon* 192). However, Bella's addiction to Jacob is only temporary. Just as the pieces which were left of her broken heart "clicked silently into place, like two corresponding puzzle pieces" (*New Moon* 116) when she sees Jacob for the first time after Edward left, she also feels "the splintering along the fissure line in my heart as the smaller part wrenched itself away from the whole" (*Eclipse* 469) the moment she realizes that there is the possibility of a future with Jacob. Nevertheless, Bella is aware of the fact that she is incapable of living without Edward.

Meyer's use of drugs and addiction as a motif is innovative as there is no other pretextual evidence that the motif was ever used in the context of a star-crossed love theme before. Nonetheless, the author applies this motif to point out another conception of love that is at the same time as irreversible and life-changing as a star-crossed love. The concept of imprinting is described as rare and limited only to the shape-shifters and their soul mates as it does not happen to ordinary humans. Based on the biologically-determined imprinting that normally takes place among animals, Meyer applies the idea of imprinting to the shape-shifting wolves which underlines their animalistic nature.

As another idea of tremendously strong and irrevocable love, imprinting is repeatedly put into contrast with the star-crossed love that Bella and Edward share. Bella compares her relationship with Edward to Sam and Emily's love and sees it as equally strong: "The way he looked at her ... well, it reminded me of a look I'd seen sometimes in Edward's eyes – when he was looking at me" (*Eclipse* 105). Meyer's use of the drug and addiction motif to communicate the significance of the connection between Jacob and Renesmee as an unconventional, fateful love enhances its status in the comparison with Edward and Bella's feelings for one another. Jacob "could feel the addiction sucking at me, trying to keep me near" (*Breaking Dawn* 181) as the unborn child within Bella draws him in. It is precisely this form of addiction to the beloved one that makes him unable to "resist another hit of my dwindling drug supply" (*Breaking Dawn* 222). Nevertheless, Jacob realizes that it is not Bella whom he has to "quit [...] cold turkey" (*Breaking Dawn* 181) but it is her belly as "the hold she had on me only got harder to break. Almost like it was related to her expanding belly – as if by getting bigger, she was gaining gravitational force" (*Breaking Dawn* 271-72). Through the expansion of the drug motif on Jacob and Renesmee, Meyer enforces the irreversibility of their love and the inseparability of the lovers, thus attempting to valorize that form of love more deeply.

However, Meyer also hints at Shakespeare's *A Midsummer Night's Dream* as the pretextual source for her concept of imprinting and one of its crucial components, the sudden falling in love that does not necessarily occur at first sight, indeed appears to have its foundation in the Shakespearean comedy. Meyer makes a direct reference to the play when she lets Edward illustrate the peculiarities of imprinting as it "reminds me of *A Midsummer Night's Dream* with all the chaos caused by the fairies' love spells ... like magic" (*Eclipse* 371). Bella, too, refers to Edward's comment on the similarities between Shakespeare's play and the concept of imprinting when she discusses it with Jacob (*Breaking Dawn* 174). Similar to the fairies in Shakespeare's play, who cast spells on the different pairs of lovers so that they all of a sudden fall for somebody completely different, it is the transformation into a wolf that triggers the process of imprinting. For Jared "it was just a girl he'd sat next to in school every day for a year and never looked at twice. And then, after he changed, he saw her again and never looked away" (*Eclipse* 111). Although what Jared and Kim experience is not a love at first sight, it is almost as intensive as the love between Edward and Bella as Edward acknowledges that "it's very nearly as strong as the way I feel about you" (*Eclipse* 371). Furthermore, both types of love seem to be like a revelation to the ones who feel them as also Jared, similarly to Edward, behaves "like a blind man seeing the sun for the first time" (*Eclipse* 215). Jared and also Edward look at their respective partner "with the incredulous eyes of first love. It would always be that way" (*Midnight Sun* 109). Additionally, also the concept of imprinting is biologically determined as it serves the means of procreation. The author makes the impact that Shakespeare's play holds on the concept of imprinting further clear through the adoption of a direct quotation from Shakespeare's comedy in the paratext of Book Jacob in *Breaking Dawn* alluding to the illogicality of love: "And yet, to say the truth, reason and love keep little company together nowadays" (*Breaking Dawn* 129). Moreover, this direct intertextual reference makes assumptions about the irrationality of Jacob's prospective beloved one.

Meyer's conception of the star-crossed lovers theme largely relies on the representation of the topos in *Wuthering Heights* and *Romeo and Juliet*. Many of the conventional characteristics of star-crossed love can be traced in the *Twilight* series and they also intertextually relate to their pretexts. Meyer's construction of the love between her protagonists similarly to its composition in Shakespeare's and Brontë's work is evident in its capacity to be all-consuming and driven by fate. Nevertheless, Meyer's depiction of Bella and Edward's first encounter is innovative as it does not resemble any conventional concept of love at first sight. Marked by numerous instances of misunderstanding the emergence of their love is characterized through first smell and physical touch. Although Meyer's use of symbols is highly intertextual, she is able to add another layer through the implementation of a drug and addiction motif that is new in the context of the ill-fated lovers. Her concept of imprinting, although intertextually inspired by *A Midsummer Night's Dream*, is innovative in its position as a contrary idea to the star-crossed lovers.

5.2.3. Sexuality and the Monster it creates

Stephenie Meyer adds another important component to the theme of the star-crossed lovers by discussing the fatalities of sexuality and abstinence and the monstrous consequences this can bring into being. Especially the implications of an active sexuality are a common point of concern in the saga as it is denied and delayed on the one side, while being openly acted out in other instances. Bella and Edward's relationship is characterized by short moments of delayed physical intimacy and long periods of abstinence creating a strong contrast to relationships like Victoria and Riley's which is exclusively based on sexual intercourse and not effectual and deceptive.

Within the concept of star-crossed love sexuality and sexual intercourse appear to be integral to the lovers' relationship. Whereas for Shakespeare's ill-fated lovers the tragic twist is triggered through the penetration of the public sphere into the lovers' private life, it is for Bella and Edward, finally, the consummation of their love that results in the ultimate conflicts that they have to overcome. Bella's pregnancy concludes in the death of her mortal body. She is aware of the fact and "not planning on surviving this human" (*Breaking Dawn* 175). Bella's "emergency vampirization" (*Breaking Dawn* 175) fits into Carlisle's scheme of saving lives as "it was that or death. He doesn't end lives, he saves them" (*Breaking Dawn* 175).

Whereas Bella eventually shies away from dying to be with Edward eternally, it is her pregnancy and her child that trigger her decision to die in the end. While Bella dies out of love to her child, Romeo and Juliet are instantly determined to take away their own lives in order to be with the respective person in death. Unable to bear even the shortest moments without the other one it is Juliet who immediately tries to kiss the remaining poison from Romeo's lips in the hope that "haply some poison yet doth hang on them" (*Romeo and Juliet* V.3.165). Cathy and Heathcliff, too, are unable to fully act out their love during their lifetimes. Shakespeare's and Brontë's star-crossed lovers are only capable of being entirely together past their own deaths. Similarly, Bella's death provides the basis for an equal relationship with her beloved one, thus indicating the necessity of death in order to overcome the final obstacles to their bonding.

Furthermore, it is the final consummation of physical intimacy that evokes the parallels between Meyer's *Breaking Dawn* and its pretexts. As such Meyer bases core elements of the forth book in her tetralogy on Polanski's *Rosemary's Baby* and Mary Shelley's Gothic novel *Frankenstein*. Both works display the possibilities and dangers that lurk in the creation of something new and unknown that can be threatening but also innovative at the same time. It is especially on the structural level that *Breaking Dawn* resembles Polanski's and Shelley's work as Bella's pregnancy and the consequent accouchement not only result in the death of her mortal body but also in the birth of a baby that arouses fear and the anxiety of the unknown. Similarly, it also provokes a fear for the baby, whose character and prospective talents are unknown, since especially Rosalie and Esme intensely care for its life and safety because they have always wanted a child of their own.

The fear of the baby is most efficiently displayed through Jacob's narration of the events and through the various vampires including the Volturi who distance themselves and repeatedly distrust Renesmee. The source of the Volturi's rejection of Bella and Edward's child and of the dangers that they project on it, an attitude displayed by the majority of vampires who meet Renesmee, is partially due to the story of the immortal children but is also based on the fear of the unknown as neither Amun nor Alistair are willing to let Renesmee touch them (*Breaking Dawn* 565, 567). Although at first unintended and without the exact knowledge of its possibility Bella consciously decides in favor of her unborn child. The creation of a vampire hybrid resembles the unlikely conception presented in Polanski's movie adaptation of *Rosemary's Baby*. Rosemary's improbable bearing of a child that is in fact supposed to have been fathered by the devil appears to be strongly irrational although displaying the insecurities and anxieties that can come up during pregnancy. Despite the fact that both women function as initiators of the sexual intimacy with their partners, the unconventional circumstances of Rosemary's pregnancy are kept secret from her for quite a long time. On the contrary, it only takes Bella minutes to realize that Edward obviously has the capability to father a child.

Although it is entirely unclear to Rosemary in how far the unusual conception of her baby has an impact on her personal constitution and whether she will survive the process of giving birth – even her friend Hutch is killed in the attempt to help her – she never puts her unborn child at any risk. Comparably, Bella is aware of the dangers that being pregnant with a half-vampire baby pose to her human body but she is willing to sacrifice her life for the child she loves: "The girl was a classic martyr. She'd totally been born in the wrong century" (*Breaking Dawn* 172). Jacob's perspective at this point displays Bella's own growing monstrosity during her pregnancy as well as it mirrors her isolation from others due to her decision to have her child.

The role that Bella takes up at this point is prototypical as she volunteers to be a mother ready to suffer for her child's well-being. She even goes beyond her own limits by feeding the fetus with blood – a substance that she herself is initially incapable of bearing as she would "faint at the sight of blood" (*Twilight* 84). The feeding of her unborn child by means of human blood as well as her own life strength – an image that intertextually has its origin in the allegorical Christian symbol of the mother pelican which feeds its young with its blood to save them from starvation or to revitalize them from the dead in return for its life – already displays Bella's transition to the fantastic other as she is no longer disgusted by blood but adopts that characteristic from her half-vampire baby: "Her expression was ... apologetic. Pleading. Scared. 'It *tastes* good'" (*Breaking Dawn* 230).

Even though Meyer does not make any overt intertextual references to Polanski's movie adaptation, Bella's pregnancy and her attitude towards her child strongly resemble Rosemary Woodhouse's final acceptance and embrace of the other in her child. Moreover, both protagonists experience their first encounters with their impending pregnancy in dreams. Bella repeatedly dreams about a little baby boy whom she desperately craves to protect from a group of cloaked attackers foreshadowing the threat through the Volturi. In her dream Bella "was struck with such a powerful need to save the lovely, terrified child" (*Breaking Dawn* 33) although already in the dream the baby is a "vampire child with […] bloodred eyes that sat on a pile of dead people I loved" (*Breaking Dawn* 95). The fact that the child Bella is going to carry is somewhat other, not to say a vampiric baby, is made obvious through her dreams and also her determination to protect the baby from every attacker is extensively displayed.

Similarly, Rosemary Woodhouse finds out about the abnormal insemination in one of her nightmares in which she is impregnated by her husband Guy who dissolves into the devil. While Bella is never even slightly terrified by the half-monster that she carries in her belly, it is Rosemary who appears strongly plagued by her baby's otherness which she repeatedly tries to deny but finally has to acknowledge that "this is no dream, this is really happening"[130]. In Polanski's film as well as in Meyer's fourth novel nightmares function as ways of introducing the monstrosity of pregnancy and sexual intercourse.

Both women eventually give birth to their children: Rosemary in a very much traditional way and Bella in a manner that inevitably kills her mortal body as she "vomited a fountain of blood" (*Breaking Dawn* 319) and gets her bones and her spine broken as "sharp snaps and cracks kept time with the spasms" (*Breaking Dawn* 320). Indeed, it is only due to Edward's fast reaction to insert his venom into multiple parts of her body that eventually saves her. The process of literally putting Bella back together – an action that is intertextually linked to the Egyptian myth of Isis and Osiris in which Isis puts the dead parts of Osiris' corpse back together in order to reanimate her husband – displays Edward's immense love for Bella and his acceptance of her choices.

Nevertheless, it is Bella who acknowledges and accepts her prospective role as mother to a vampire hybrid right from the commencement of her pregnancy: "I wanted him like I wanted air to breathe. Not a choice – a necessity" (*Breaking Dawn* 120). Meanwhile, Rosemary does not want to take up the role as the baby's mother until the final scene of the movie in which she eventually accepts her maternal role. Whereas Rosemary experiences a natural process of pregnancy and is terrified by its unnatural outcome, it is precisely this unnatural devolution and the child's otherness that Bella appreciates and desires: "I didn't really care about having a baby. I didn't even think about it. It's not just having a baby. It's ... well ... *this* baby" (*Breaking Dawn* 177). The longing for her monstrous child determines her willingness to transcend to the other as she is evidently ready to leave her human life behind. As such Bella's pregnancy also functions as an indicator of her subtle transition into the realms of the other, thus foreshadowing her impending transformation into a vampire.

The notion of mothering that Meyer's heroine adopts right from the beginning of her pregnancy and that again and again resurfaces after her transmutation is a feeling that she primarily shares with Esme and moreover at this point of the story, even with Rosalie. It displays a natural female emotion that Meyer inverts through its disposition on a number of female vampires which has been uncharacteristic to fantastic creatures so far. However, mothering also appears as an unnatural reaction for the protagonist as it is eventually her own child and the process of giving birth to it which kills her mortal body. The horrors and

---

[130] *Rosemary's Baby,* dir. Roman Polanski, perfs. Mia Farrow, John Cassavetes, Ruth Gordon, and Sidney Blackmer, 1968, DVD, Paramount Pictures, 2001.

anxieties of pregnancy are, however, mostly expressed and articulated through the male vampires as well as Jacob in the *Twilight* series. The inversion of female emotions that takes place in the saga stands in contradiction to *Rosemary's Baby* in which the horrors of pregnancy are entirely expressed by Rosemary.

In *Rosemary's Baby* the monster emerges from within the nuclear family and similarly in Meyer's work it does, too. As the consequence of a successful impregnation Renesmee functions as the trigger to take Edward and Bella's relationship to a level where both can regard the respective partner as equal as Bella's pregnancy makes her final transformation inevitable. Comparably, the final scene of Polanski's movie shows Rosemary eventually accepting her baby and becoming a true mother to it. Also the conflict between her and her husband Guy is resolved as her fear of him is diminished to a great extend and is replaced by the love and care that she now expresses for the baby.

Whereas notions of fear for the baby can be traced back to *Rosemary's Baby*, it is precisely the fear of the unknown and monstrous in *Breaking Dawn* that bears similarities to Mary Shelley's *Frankenstein*. Although Meyer once again does not provide any overt intertextual references to Shelley's Gothic novel the features both works have in common are numerous. In both novels it is the creation of a new individual that brings about anxieties and moments of fear. Bella and Edward's child is begotten through the natural act of physical intimacy and acted out sexuality while Frankenstein's monster is created without any female participation. In the Creature's vitalization Frankenstein ignores the maternal role of women in his desperate attempt to bring new life into being, thus trying to create a new species that "would bless me as its creator and source" (*Frankenstein* 32). However, he cannot and the result of his creation is disastrous as Frankenstein condemns his Creature at first sight: "I had selected his features as beautiful [...] but now that I had finished, the beauty of the dream vanished, and breathless horror and disgust filled my heart" (*Frankenstein* 34).

Both works address the issue of repulsion towards beings that are considered threatening and unfamiliar. Shelley illustrates this notion right from the beginning as even Frankenstein is incapable of accepting his creation, regretting "the demoniacal corpse to which I had so miserably given life" (*Frankenstein* 35) even before it has committed any crime at all. Again and again he ignores his Creature's claim to being an individual by denying the act of name-giving as well as gender specification to it. Similarly, Jacob is unable to refer to Bella's unborn child by any ordinary name thus calling it, like Sam does, monster or vampire "spawn" (*Breaking Dawn* 163, 194) in order to denote their repudiation for it. He also repeatedly addresses the unborn Renesmee as a neutral entity relating to her as an "it" and hence depriving her of any claim to being regarded as human or at least worth living.

Due to the society in which Frankenstein's monster regains life it is immediately repelled because of its monstrous, inhumane looks. Without ever being offered the chance to explain its origin or receiving any tribute for the unselfish help, as it grants relief to the De Lacey family, it is entirely excluded. Comparably, Renesmee is initially repudiated by a number of people because of the threat she poses to her mother as even "Edward had a difficult time using a term as mild as *fetus*" (*Breaking Dawn* 220). None of the Cullens is even sure about what exactly Bella is carrying as "there's never been anything like Bella and I before. How could we know that a human was able to conceive a child with one of us" (*Breaking Dawn* 164). This fear of the unknown and unfamiliar is further enhanced through the pain the baby causes Bella during the condensed time of pregnancy as "her stomach looked like it was stained with big splotches of purple-black ink" (*Breaking Dawn* 178). Edward and Jacob are left to be mere spectators without any possibility to help which results in the intensification of their anger.

As Renesmee gains acceptance within the Cullen family and among the shape-shifters other vampires avoid her nonetheless. While some vampires simply refuse to touch her and react to her "like a human confronted by a venomous snake" (*Breaking Dawn* 542), others cross her path with insurmountable horror and fear. Renesmee's resemblance with the immortal children and Bella's realization that the Volturi's witnesses "wanted to help tear and burn" (*Breaking Dawn* 633) her family, displays the prejudices that they have to face. Similarly, Frankenstein's Creature has to deal with repeated animosity and repudiation that causes and determines its later behavior towards other individuals and human society as everyone else "were at rest or in enjoyment: I, like the arch fiend, bore a hell within me" (*Frankenstein* 92). While Frankenstein's Creature illustrates the guilt society bears in the development of its character and eventually results in the fear of the monster, Bella and Edward's daughter does not personally generate any animosity by her actions. It is her unusual status as a half-vampire combined with the vampire world's fear of the immortal children that causes terror.

Meyer's covert intertextual references to Polanski's movie adaptation of *Rosemary's Baby* and Shelley's *Frankenstein* are primarily of structural significance as they give directions to the novel's final conflict. Although the author does not supply any overt markers, pretextual references are capable of achieving an enhanced illustration of the monstrous fear that originates from Bella's abnormal conception and her unusual half-and-half child. Moreover, the horrors of the female reproductive process are intensively addressed through the incorporation of *Rosemary's Baby*. However, intertextual references to Meyer's pretexts appear hard to grasp for the reader due to the lack of direct quotation or any other straightforward allusions to the texts. Although similarities to Polanski's as well as Shelley's works pervade the entire plot of *Breaking Dawn*, Meyer does not seem to be aware of these influences. Consequently, she only notes Shakespeare's *A Midsummer Night's Dream* and *The Merchant of Venice* – she drew the denouement for the final conflict from Shakespeare's play[131] – as sources for her work on the fourth book of the tetralogy, thus diminishing the intertextual potential of *Rosemary's Baby* and *Frankenstein*.

5.3. DOUBLING FIGURES

Apart from Meyer's adoption of the prominent vampire motif and the theme of the star-crossed lovers, a deployment of other already established conventions can also be assumed. Meyer makes use of the literary heroic tradition through the use of the Byronic hero in the character of Edward as well as a number of other motifs such as the *femme fatale*. This evokes that other characters could have the capability for intertextual potential, too. Besides the positioning of multitudinous explicit as well as numerous covert references to her pretexts in her novels, she also employs characters who are conscious of their pretextual heritage and put their own actions in relation to their predecessors. Bella as well as Edward are firmly aware of the parallels they evoke with star-crossed lovers like Romeo and Juliet or Heathcliff and Cathy.

 A further analysis on the basis of other characters as well as the structural composition of the *Twilight* series seems relevant. It will be necessary to take a closer look at Bella while she is still human and Renée, who has not been discussed within an intertextual framework so far. Furthermore, structural elements such as letters, notes, and newspaper articles that have as yet not been mentioned will be analyzed and put into an intertextual context as they serve as narrative devices in Meyer's work.

---

[131] According to Meyer's FAQ section on *Breaking Dawn* on her webpage "Alice tore a page from *The Merchant of Venice* because the end of *Breaking Dawn* was going to be somewhat familiar": Stephenie Meyer, "Frequently Asked Questions: *Breaking Dawn*," *The Official Website of Stephenie Meyer*, 5 October 2010, 7 October 2010 <http://www.stepheniemeyer.com/bd_faq.html>.

5.3.1. Doubling Characters

The procedure of doubling characters is an effort that Meyer has utilized in her *Twilight* saga at various instances. Her positioning of Edward Cullen as a twenty-first-century exemplar of the Byronic hero and the diversified depictions of female vampires as *femmes fatales* as well as caring, loving mothers that Meyer creates in her work evokes the assumption that also other characters are endowed with intertextual potential. While the presentation of the Byronic hero and the construction of the motif of the *femme fatale* are restricted to the vampiric characters in the series, other human figures such as Bella and her mother Renée also have the capability to be intertextually relevant.

Bella's outward appearance illustrates the numerous parallels between Meyer's heroine and the nineteenth-century motif of the *femme fragile*. Characterized through a girl's weakness, fragility, and morbidity the motif was exceedingly prominent in aesthetic literature. Most notably, Bella's weak constitution reminds the reader of that particular character type as she "had always been slender, but soft somehow" (*Twilight* 9) and "looked sallower, unhealthy" (*Twilight* 9) since she moved to Forks. Her skin is described as "clear, almost translucent-looking" (*Twilight* 9) and uncharacteristic for someone being raised in Phoenix, Arizona. Already Bella's outward appearance displays her physical frailty.

When Edward leaves Bella behind in Forks she becomes mentally unstable and starts to imagine hearing Edward's voice. However, his absence also affects her physically. Bella realizes that her emotionless behavior makes her "wind up as a *zombie*" (*New Moon* 95) as she is initially unable to enjoy life to any extent before she meets up with Jacob. However, not only Bella's behavior changes without Edward's presence but Bella also alters tremendously in her outward appearance. Besides the already pale complexion of her skin her entire appearance seems unhealthy, almost dead and zombie-like:

> Even my outsides looked different – my face sallow, white except for the purple circles the nightmares had left under my eyes. My eyes were dark enough against my pallid skin that – if I were beautiful and seen from a distance – I might even pass for a vampire now. (*New Moon* 110)

Bella is at this point linked to the undead in her physical appearance. Although vampires in Meyer's series are displayed as invincible and beautiful the dark shadows under their eyes (*Twilight* 16) are remnants of their undead nature and the blackness of Bella's eyes evokes similarities to Meyer's vampires. Her unhealthy appearance links Bella once again to the *femme fragile* as she looks closer to the dead than to the living – a feature that also characterizes the fragile woman of aesthetic literature with her ailing complexion that

100

repeatedly reminds one of consumption. Moreover, also Edward initially views her as a "frail woman-child" (*Midnight Sun* 14).

Apart from her obviously pale complexion Bella's overly displayed clumsiness contributes to her status as a *femme fragile*. It further enhances her fragile constitution as she is prone to fall and get bruises so she would even need "every ounce of concentration to make it down the icy brick driveway" (*Twilight* 46) without tripping and falling. Since "she can't walk across a flat, stable surface without finding something to trip over" (*Twilight* 186) Edward denies Bella the ability to keep herself safe and sound. Furthermore, it increases the possibility to be involved in accidents as she even trips "several times, once falling, catching myself with my hands" (*Twilight* 386) while she is on her way to the ballet studio to meet James.

During her life as a human Bella's obvious inability to protect herself and her family, as well as the sentiment of vulnerability and necessity for protection that Edward transports onto her without her initial consent, trigger notions of the damsel in distress – a maiden who is repeatedly exposed to dangerous situations or villains and thus needs a protector to save her life as her own attempts are ineffectual and naïve. Meyer turns her heroine into a damsel in distress – a stock character in fiction ever since the Middle Ages with contemporary successors such as Lois Lane from the *Superman* movies. Bella is already sufficiently challenged by a number of absolutely ordinary accidents like the repeated motorcycle crashes in which she is involved. Her attempts at defending herself are completely ineffectual, thus illustrating her need for a protector. When she tries to fend off the rapists in Port Angeles by means of her purse her actions are only marginally helpful and would have been entirely inefficient without Edward's intervention.

Besides the maiden's helplessness and necessity to be rescued from monsters or villains, the rescuer's motives for saving the young woman are essential. Generally, besides the fact that the hero evidently has to exhibit a grand potential for superhuman strength to save the damsel, his intentions need to be heroic and free of any hidden agenda as only that justifies the rescuer's deeds and proves his moral goodness. Edward's actions in saving Bella's life after James sucked her blood and thus triggered Bella's transformation into a vampire are entirely warrantable as his motives to give her a chance at a human life – a decision that he repeatedly does not want to take away from her – are heroic. Likewise, Jacob rescues Bella when she is about to drown as he assumes Edward's position as her protector and rescuer while he is away.

Moreover, Bella's deficient sense of orientation displays her need for assistance and support as her "sense of direction was hopeless; I could get lost in much less helpful surroundings" (*Twilight* 118). Although her lack of orientation does not get the heroine into any dangerous situations, it nonetheless illustrates her inability to keep herself safe as the author does not necessarily have to bring up villains who persecute her because she is capable of getting into trouble all by herself. Repeatedly, Meyer describes Bella as too fragile and breakable to manage and overcome the hazards of a world full of superhuman creatures. It is consequently Edward who has to fill the role of her protector: "The delicate framework of her bones, the thin sheath of her pale skin – like silk stretched over glass, incredibly soft and easy to shatter. She was too vulnerable for this world. She *needed* a protector" (*Midnight Sun* 192).

Whereas the character of Bella Swan is consistently depicted as fragile as well as soft and serves as an example of the motifs of the *femme fragile* and the damsel in distress, it is Bella's mother, Renée, who represents the type of the anti-mother. She functions as a mere friend, rather than an actual mother, to her daughter. Bella feels comfortable talking with her, unlike with her father, about almost everything as "it wasn't embarrassing with my mom. After all, I'd been the one giving her that lecture time and time again in the last ten years" (*Eclipse* 60). Consequently, as a friend it is also not surprising that she would get Bella "Victoria's Secret silk pajamas" (*Twilight* 140) for her sixteenth birthday. Moreover, Renée is depicted as a mother who is incapable of fulfilling the basic duties of that role as Bella "did the shopping at home, and […] fell into the pattern of the familiar task gladly" (*Twilight* 28). Besides Renée's inability to nourish her daughter as she "was an imaginative cook, and her experiments weren't always edible" (*Twilight* 30), Bella also has to take responsibility for her own mother and to remind her of things (*Twilight* 29).

Renée not only denies her own role as a parent for Bella when she rather travels around the country with her new husband than taking care of her child, but she has also been incapable of acting as a parent since Bella's childhood. When Renée visits Bella at the hospital after James' attack in Phoenix she is concerned about her daughter's relationship with Edward as it "was the first time since I was eight that she'd come close to trying to sound like a parental authority" (*Twilight* 407).

Behaving at times more like she herself is the child and not the mother, Renée is furthermore described as "irresponsible and slightly eccentric" (*Twilight* 90) as well as "loving, erratic, harebrained" (*Twilight* 4) by Bella. This is further displayed by her unwillingness to spend the nights at her own house since the ballet studio burned down and "there's been some crime in the neighborhood, and I don't like being there alone" (*Twilight* 408). Moreover, Renée is characterized as incapable of fending for herself as she needs her new husband, Phil, to take care of her so that "the bills would probably get paid, there would be food in the refrigerator, gas in her car, and someone to call when she got lost" (*Twilight* 4). She is described as very curious – only barely able to conceal "the raging curiosity in her voice" (*Twilight* 407) when questioning Bella about Edward – and talkative, in opposition to Charlie, because to leave her daughter alone in her new room is "a feat that would have been altogether impossible for my mother" (*Twilight* 8). Besides these character traits and thus creating a strong contrast to Bella's responsible nature, Renée is also characterized as passionate and getting easily absorbed when she plays the piano as "she seemed like a new, mysterious being to me then, someone outside the 'mom' persona I took for granted" (*Twilight* 284). Nonetheless, she is pictured as excessively imprudent, forgetting "how paralyzed she was by heights until she was already strapped to a parachute and a dive instructor" (*Eclipse* 39).

Another instance of an anti-mother is illustrated in Jane Austen's *Pride and Prejudice* through the character of Elizabeth's mother. Most of the time occupied with the coupling of her five daughters Mrs. Bennet appears not only thoroughly narrow-minded and repeatedly frivolous in her propositions and actions but also explicitly articulates the necessity for a young woman to find a suitable husband and secure her livelihood. More than Renée, Mrs. Bennet is pictured as uncaring and unreasonable when it comes to Elizabeth's and Jane's concerns, blaming Elizabeth as "the real cause of all the mischief" (*Pride and Prejudice* 109) when Mr. Collins decides to marry Elizabeth's friend Charlotte. Additionally, Mrs. Bennet is completely unaware of her daughter's feelings when she eventually falls in love with Darcy and later on only considers his fortune amiable (*Pride and Prejudice* 316). Being the one who is mostly at fault for her younger daughters' misconduct she is incapable of conveying proper demeanor to them, consequently repeatedly embarrassing her older daughters with her own behavior. Similarly, Elizabeth and Jane appear to be more mature and better adapted to the society in which they dwell than their own mother, finally taking full responsibility for themselves and choosing their prospective husbands without Mrs. Bennet's interference.

Bella, who is displayed as a *femme fragile* only in her outward appearance, is characterized as a fully-fledged damsel in distress in her actions and needs for a protector until she is eventually transformed into a vampire. Accordingly, Meyer repeatedly describes her protagonist as delicate and breakable and lets her endure dangerous situations in which she is in need of protection to save her life, thereby enhancing the intertextual effect of the motif. Comparably, Meyer again and again refers to her heroine's worry about her mother Renée, emphasizing the reversed mother-daughter relationship that they have. Although Renée is depicted as an anti-mother who does not fulfill the role of the caring parent sufficiently, she is, contrary to Mrs. Bennet, able to see the concerns of her daughter and acts according to Bella's feelings while Elizabeth's mother fails at this throughout. Intertextually, Meyer is therefore able to create in Renée an anti-mother that clearly differentiates oneself from Austen's Mrs. Bennet as she still understands her daughter's single most important feelings whereas both mothers leave their daughters to care for themselves.

5.3.2. Doubling Structures

Relying on the plots of works like Austen's *Pride and Prejudice*, Shakespeare's *Romeo and Juliet* as well as Bronte's *Wuthering Heights* Meyer has composed her *Twilight* series to be structurally intertextual. By means of frequent direct and indirect pretextual references to her pretexts she is able to construct her novels by utilizing her sources as structural layers for her own composition, thus creating her texts according to her sources. Nevertheless, Meyer's reliance on her pretexts goes even further as she adopts other significant structural components from pretextual sources.

In her tetralogy, Meyer repeatedly uses letters and notes to convey information from one character to another. This is especially evident when taking a closer look at the love triangle between Bella, Edward, and Jacob. Edward wants Bella to take care of herself while he is away for a hunting trip or copies Bella's handwriting to let her father know where to look for her after he leaves her alone in the woods. In almost the same manner Bella communicates with Edward at school when she wants to find out what happened between the Cullens and the shape-shifters in Forks while they were away visiting Renée in Florida. But also Jacob lets the heroine know through messages delivered by Charlie that he is unwilling to further meet Bella due to the ancestral conflict between vampires and werewolves. Additionally, Edward communicates the invitation to their wedding in a letter which leads to Jacob's disappearance for a couple of weeks. Likewise, Bella repeatedly interacts with her mother via e-mails conveying news that they want to share with the other one.

Whereas Meyer only uses letters and notes in her novels on occasion, Bram Stoker's Gothic novel *Dracula* is entirely designed as an epistolary novel consisting of numerous diary entries and letters from one character to another. This type of the novel which Stoker adopts for his vampire tale conveys a large amount of instantaneousness as most of the diary entries are constructed to appear to be written immediately after the occurrence of the events that are narrated in the entries. Moreover, this form of immediacy leads to the increase of suspense as events like Dracula sucking Mina's blood seem to have happened only recently. A sense of directness is conferred on to the reader, providing him with a notion of events that have just occurred.

Comparably, Meyer inserts letters and notes which her characters exchange that have the capability to convey situations and events as instantaneous. These messages also display the characters' feelings towards others or the conflicts they find themselves in. The worries that battle within Jacob for example are evident in his note to Bella in *Eclipse* saying that he cannot see her anymore. It consists of a number of crossed out sentences illustrating Jacob's interior struggle to see Bella as well as the dislike that he feels for the vampires. Additionally, Meyer endows Bella, Edward and Jacob with a characteristic handwriting which stays with the characters throughout the entire tetralogy. Edward is given an "elegant script" (*Twilight* 218) that appears especially filigree and "fancy" (*Eclipse* 556). Due to his vampiric nature and his subsequent skills he is also capable of copying Bella's "messy handwriting" (*New Moon* 73), imitating it just as accurately as she does it herself. Therefore, Meyer not only inserts letters and notes composed by a limited number of her characters but also endows them with typographical characteristics – sometimes like in Jacob's writing, even adding multiple spots of ink – that are specific for every character. By this means Meyer is able to achieve her own form of instantaneousness, thus conveying closeness to reality.

Meyer also makes wide use of newspaper articles as well as headlines in the third volume of her *Twilight* tetralogy in order to inform the major characters and her readers about the incidents of the vampire newborns in Seattle. This also serves to expedit the threat the newborns pose to the protagonists. The newspaper headline "Death Toll on the Rise, Police fear Gang Activity" (*Eclipse* 22) triggers Edward and Bella's discussion of what is going on in Seattle and introduces the topic of newborn vampires and their thirstiness for blood. Similarly, it is an advertising flyer saying "Save the Olympic Wolf" (*Eclipse* 88) that eventually makes Bella visit Jacob in La Push, thus renewing their friendship. Accentuated through the use of a different, distinct font Meyer endows these headlines with the capacity to provide information, evoke actions, but also to convey a strong sense of immediacy. Moreover, these pre-eminent headlines communicate notions of reality as Meyer makes the newspaper headlines appear in the *Seattle Times* (*Eclipse* 203), thus giving them an undisputable reference to reality.

Additionally, she inserts an entire newspaper article with the title "Seattle terrorized by Slayings" (*Eclipse* 247) on the killings in the largest city nearby in her third novel. This intensifies the danger that the newborns pose to the protagonists as "the motive seems to be killing for no other reason than to kill" (*Eclipse* 248). Through the matter-of-fact style that is common for newspaper articles and the illustration of numerous gory details since the article also notes that "twenty-two have occurred in the last 10 days alone" (*Eclipse* 249), Meyer repeatedly achieves moments of actuality. Thence, she intertwines elements of the real world with the fictional story she narrates.

Comparably, Stoker includes newspaper articles in his epistolary novel, endowing his work with notions of actuality to communicate information about his villain to his characters and readers. The article from *The Pall Mall Gazette*, an evening newspaper read in nineteenth-century London, inferentially relates the news of an escaped wolf from the zoological gardens (*Dracula* 125-29), thus hinting at Dracula's powers that are also threatening in England. Likewise, an article from the *Dailygraph* which is pasted into Mina's Journal reports on the mysterious incidents of the arrival of the Demeter in Whitby followed by an extract from the log of the ship relating the disappearance of the sailors. The newspaper articles that Stoker employs in *Dracula* serve to convey actions that cannot be related by means of the characters' letters, journal entries or telegrams as the characters do not participate in these actions. Similarly, Bella finds out about the killings in Seattle through newspaper articles as these actions take place outside of her own perspective. At this point Meyer adopts precisely the same technique that Stoker already uses in his Gothic novel as she is at this moment bound to Bella's perspective to narrate the story.

Whereas letters, notes as well as newspaper headings and articles denote instantaneousness and actuality, instances of analepses as well as prolepses and the framing of narrated events shed additional light on the characters' motives and actions. The causes for Rosalie and Esme's maternal instincts are laid out which ultimately vindicate their supportive behavior towards Bella during her pregnancy. Similarly, Emmett's desire to repeatedly battle against bears and defeat them is rooted in his human past and his transformation into a vampire. Rosalie gives an account of that story for Bella, thus presenting the reasons for Emmett's choice of favorite prey. Comparably, Mary Shelley presents her readers with a number of frame narratives that take up the function of analepsis. Walton, the Arctic mariner, whose letters to his sister open and close the narrative of *Frankenstein* relates the story of the creator and his Creature and displays Frankenstein's motivation in committing the terrible deed of bringing a new creature into being. In addition, the narration of the Creature's own actions appears distinctly monstrous but also evokes sympathy for the Creature's miserable fortune in the reader.

Meyer's use of analepses is, compared to its employment in Shelley's Gothic novel, limited. Whereas, *Frankenstein* due to the structural framing of independent narratives consists to a large part of analepses couched into the form of an epistolary novel, Meyer's use of this narrative device is to display and make her characters' motives and decision comprehensible. Another narrative device can be detected in both works that does not take the narrative back in time but forward to a prospective point in the story. The proleptic dreams that Meyer inserts as a plot device in her *Twilight* series hint at upcoming situations that her protagonist has to face. This is most evident in Bella's foreshadowing dream of her baby's origin as a half-being which she experiences various times. Although Shelley only endows her protagonist with one single dream in which Frankenstein imagines his prospective wife Elizabeth dead (*Frankenstein* 34), it is this dream that displays great foretelling qualities as the scientist, indeed, will find his wife dead on the day of their marriage.

Meyer's display of plot devices ranging from letters and notes with fonts that are specific to every particular character, to newspaper articles and headings as well as the deployment of analepses and prolepses show intertextual potential. Although these techniques are conventional and already apparent in earlier narratives, Meyer's use of *Dracula* and *Frankenstein* as pretexts suggests that her adoption of the devices discussed above is influenced by these two Gothic novels. As such, these narrative devices are intertextual potent signifying instantaneousness and immediacy as they enhance the texts' suspense.

6. The *Twilight* Saga – An Intertextual Summary

As could be shown through the preceding analysis intertextual references within Meyer's *Twilight* tetralogy are diversified and numerous on every level of the narration. The perspective that the author applies, especially in her manuscript version of *Midnight Sun* is intertextual as it bears similarities with Mary Shelley's framed narrative of the Creature's story. The construction of Edward Cullen as the Byronic hero, too, goes along the lines of its heroic tradition. Furthermore, the depiction of female vampires as either *femmes fatales* such as Rosalie, Heidi, Victoria and the Denalis or figures with a loving maternal nature such as Esme has strong intertextual potential. In this respect Meyer implicitly goes back to the poems of Goethe, Coleridge, and Keats which all depict fatal and demonic seductresses. Representations of good and evil within the series have shown that both concepts remain fairly straightforward in their definition when it comes to a comparison of the Volturi and the Cullens. The vampire within society remains within its position as an outsider although various attempts on the side of the Cullens are made to change that status. Regarding these two points Meyer mainly makes use of Stoker's *Dracula* as her pretext. The theme of the star-crossed lovers, too, is greatly influenced by Meyer's pretextual sources. Obstacles to the lovers' relationship, the all-consuming characteristic of their love and its irreversibility are highly intertextual factors when it comes to works like Shakespeare's *Romeo and Juliet* and Brontë's *Wuthering Heights*. In fact, Meyer incorporates a vast number of overt references to these works.

Additionally, Meyer makes great use of structural layers to tell her stories as she relies on Austen's *Pride and Prejudice*, Shelley's *Frankenstein* as well as Shakespeare's plays and Brontë's novel to construct the plot, thus also incorporating other themes and motifs from these works. Every volume of Meyer's tetralogy is structurally based on at least one singular pretext. Since she repeatedly refers to her pretexts Meyer also achieves the creation of characters that are strongly intertextual. Bella, Edward, and Jacob show large potential for interfigurality as the author compares them to Juliet, Romeo, and Paris as well as Cathy, Heathcliff, and Edgar. The protagonists consciously compare themselves with their literary predecessors or present qualities which are inevitably linked to former examples of that character type. By this means, Bella recognizes similarities between herself and Cathy, thus enhancing her own interfigurality. Nonetheless, she is also portrayed as a damsel in distress while she is human. Meanwhile, Renée engages the position of the anti-mother showing parallels to Austen's Mrs. Bennet. Moreover, Meyer employs a number of structural devices like letters, notes, and newspaper articles to convey instantaneousness and to achieve an enhanced sense of immediacy – characteristics that are already evident in Stoker's *Dracula* or Shelley's *Frankenstein* which both take the form of epistolary novels.

On the other hand, Meyer is also able to create a number of characteristics that are innovative and that are not necessarily based on pretextual sources. Bella's perspective is that of a character undergoing a coded conversion leading to the transformation of the self into the other through the discovery of one's own otherness. The protagonist is incapable of fitting into the human world but only feels truly at home within the realm of the other. The perspective that Meyer applies at this point is innovative because neither Shelley nor any other author of Meyer's pretexts has adopted such a perspective. Furthermore, Meyer endows the male vampire, Edward, with the exertion of physical intimacy and physicality although this trait was originally conferred on the female vampire in nineteenth-century literature. Meyer also establishes a new concept of love that is, similarly to the star-crossed love, biologically determined, fateful and irreversible. Although inspired by Shakespeare's *A Midsummer Night's Dream* the idea of imprinting is innovative, serving as a counter concept to the protagonists' fatal love at first touch/scent.

Meyer uses a great number of intertextual references to various pretexts in her work and these markers are of varying degrees of intensity. These references are evident on various layers of the narrative ranging from already mentioned pretexts as physical objects in the story, interfigurality, intertextuality in themes and motifs to structural similarities. Again there are varying degrees of intertextual productivity extending from covert references such as specific character traits that bear similarities to former character types to overt markers such as pretexts that occur as actual objects in the fictional world of the characters. These implicit references, for example to the Byronic hero, show the significance of Byron's *Manfred* for Meyer's work although it is not apparently marked. On the other hand, distinct parts from *Romeo and Juliet* and *Wuthering Heights* are quoted in Meyer's novels and their pretextual sources are clearly named, thus evoking an immense intertextual potential.

Meyer's use of overt intertextual markers and the repeated references to the works she takes these references from open up the possibility for the average reader to recognize the author's deployment of these texts. Through direct quotations, obvious allusions as well as apparent interfigural comparisons to pretextual characters Meyer enhances her readers' capacity to realize the intertextual potential of the *Twilight* series. The influence that works like Shakespeare's *Romeo and Juliet* and Brontë's *Wuthering Heights* have on Meyer's tetralogy is self-evident through the wide variety of overt references to both works. On the other hand, covert references that are created by means of Meyer's adoption of already prominent themes, motifs, and heroic traditions remain obscure to the average reader. Left without any distinct markers to the number of Meyer's pretexts that are only implicitly bequeathed in the series an average reader is incapable of realizing the texts' full intertextual potential.

7. Conclusion

Over the past couple of years Stephenie Meyer's *Twilight* tetralogy has become the catalyst in vampire fiction, thus elevating the entire genre to a new popularity within the realm of popular culture. The vampires Meyer creates in her series display the multi-facetted nature of a creature of the fantastic that has always had the capability to illustrate various angles of human desires and fears. Closely linked to the vampire's ability as a creature of neither the living nor the dead to transgress boundaries and occupy every position in society that has been conferred on it so far is the revenant's potential for intertextuality. Through its ambiguity the figure of the vampire clearly has the capacity to be intertextually productive. A number of critics have already assumed the great capability for intertextuality in the *Twilight* series. Nevertheless, their attempts have been limited to only singular characteristics of Meyer's work and have never taken the entire tetralogy into account. As intertextuality in Meyer's works has not yet been sufficiently explored the thesis at hand analyzed the novels' intertextual potential in themes, structures, and characters in order to display Meyer's adoption of patterns and themes already prominent in earlier literary works.

Accordingly, a hermeneutic, structuralist intertextual approach was taken to systematize and describe the interrelations between Meyer's *Twilight* saga and its relevant pretexts. This has lead to a number of results. Overt as well as covert intertextual references to Meyer's pretexts are diversified throughout the tetralogy thus creating an intertextual paradigm that pervades the entire *Twilight* series. Meyer's sources are heterogeneous encompassing every literary genre and coming from different literary periods. Numerous pretextual references are distinctly marked in Meyer's work through direct quotations from the pretexts or through allusions to particular pretextual characters. Direct references that are presented in the works' paratext anticipate the texts' overall direction and put them in primary relation to the particular pretexts thus evoking strong intertextual potential. Nevertheless, there is a great number of covert references in the series that allude to specific character types or heroic traditions like the Byronic hero. These references are not particularly pointed out and are often only visible in the characters' behavior and character traits. They are not obvious to the average reader who is not familiar with specific character types or literary topoi. Likewise covert references to Shelley's *Frankenstein* as well as Polanski's movie adaptation of *Rosemary's Baby* which are influential for the construction of *Breaking Dawn* appear to be unapparent to the author, thereby diminishing their intertextual potential.

Intertextual markers are contextualized in the themes of the *Twilight* series as they repeatedly point at the themes' intertextual productivity. They form an essential constituent in the composition of themes such as the star-crossed lovers as they broaden the themes' meaning and create another dimension of understanding. Meyer similarly deals with already prominent motifs. Through a restricted number of direct markers that refer to works that handle the same motif and multiple covert references Meyer hints at the motifs' origin, thus expanding the motifs' productivity. Comparably, the potential for interfigurality is great within the tetralogy and it is essential to the protagonists' identification within the story's framework. Intertextuality is largely intensified through the protagonists' capability to reflect on their own interfigurality as they realize similarities between themselves and pretextual characters. The characters' interfigural potential is at times further enhanced through the names they are given as, for example, Edward Cullen is linked to *Jane Eyre*'s Edward Rochester by name. Other characters also bear names that denote and describe their most significant character traits. Frequently, the characters' interfigural and the texts' general intertextual capacity is intensified by the pretexts that form a physical part of Meyer's fictional world. They occur as actual books that the protagonists' read or movies they watch and eventually discuss. Other references, although mostly non-literal, allude to entire literary genres or topoi in Meyer's work as a number of parallels to the Gothic novel are evoked through allusions to Stoker's *Dracula* and Shelley's *Frankenstein*.

Meyer's pretextual references not only hint at constructing intertextuality between her texts and her sources but she also applies these markers to extend and alter her themes, motifs and characters, at times endowing them with additional characteristics. As such, her star-crossed lovers eventually have the capability to achieve a happy end and Edward as a Byronic hero has the capacity to change. Meyer's use of references leads to numerous instances of intertextuality, through which her themes, motifs, and characters are expanded and redefined. Therefore, Meyer broadens the intertextual components of her series, thus endowing them with further meaning, adapting them to a postmodern literary framework, and embedding them into a new context.

As has been already noted, intertextual approaches to Meyer's *Twilight* series have been so far only limited due to the phenomenon's novelty and critics' repeated gripping on Meyer's religious views. Whereas an expanded number of analyses on Meyer's religious motifs in the series has been published, her series' intertextual relations to other literary works has only fractionally been discussed. As such, the analysis at hand aims at making a crucial contribution within the field of intertextual studies on Meyer's work since little research has been done in this realm until the present day. However, this work can also serve as a starting point from which further research, also in the field of intertextual studies, can be carried out as Meyer's tetralogy and her subsequent works that also revolve around her *Twilight* series offer continuing potential for analysis. Especially in the field of intertextual studies there is still further capacity for research as Meyer's series has proved to be immensely productive, thus showing a great intertextual potential. As the work at hand has focused to a great extend on the postmodern vampire figure and its manifold otherness a thorough analysis of the intertextual potential of the fantastic shape-shifting werewolves could not be carried out. Nevertheless, this could serve as a point for further analysis that could be beneficial and take up an intertextual scope as well.

With the series' constant popularity among its readers, its ongoing world-wide merchandising and the ensuing increase in vampire literature further research in this genre appears to be long running. The *Twilight* saga itself offers ample potential for prospective analyses, thus ensuring the continuity of the phenomenon.

8. Bibliography

Primary Literature

Austen, Jane. *Mansfield Park*. Hertfordshire: Wordsworth Editions, 2007.

---. *Pride and Prejudice*. Hertfordshire: Wordsworth Editions, 2007.

Brontë, Charlotte. *Jane Eyre*. London: Penguin Books, 1994.

Brontë, Emily. *Wuthering Heights*. London: Penguin Books, 1994.

Byron, Lord George Gordon. "Manfred." Jack Stillinger and Deidre Shauna Lynch (eds.). *The Norton Anthology of English Literature 8th Edition: The Romantic Period*. New York: W.W. Norton & Company, 2006. 636-669.

Coleridge, Samuel Taylor. "Christabel." Jack Stillinger and Deidre Shauna Lynch (eds.). *The Norton Anthology of English Literature 8th Edition: The Romantic Period*. New York: W.W. Norton & Company, 2006. 449-464.

---. "The Rime of the Ancient Mariner." Jack Stillinger and Deidre Shauna Lynch (eds.). *The Norton Anthology of English Literature 8th Edition: The Romantic Period*. New York: W.W. Norton & Company, 2006. 430-446.

Goethe, Johann Wolfgang von. "Die Braut von Korinth." Erich Trunz (ed.). *Goethe Gedichte*. München: C. H. Beck, 1998. 268-273.

Keats, John. "Lamia." Jack Stillinger and Deidre Shauna Lynch (eds.). *The Norton Anthology of English Literature 8th Edition: The Romantic Period*. New York: W.W. Norton & Company, 2006. 910-925.

Mackenzie, Henry. *The Man of Feeling*. Brian Vickers (ed.) Oxford: Oxford University Press, 2009.

Meyer, Stephenie. *Breaking Dawn*. London: Atom Books, 2008.

---. *Eclipse*. London: Atom Books, 2007.

---. *New Moon*. London: Atom Books, 2006.

---. *The Short Second Life of Bree Tanner: An Eclipse Novella*. London: Atom Books, 2010.

---. *Twilight*. London: Atom Books, 2005.

---. "Midnight Sun." *The official Website of Stephenie Meyer*. 28.08.2008. 22.01.2010 <http://www. stepheniemeyer.com/pdf/midnightsun_partial_draft4.pdf>.

Polidori, John. "The Vampyre; a Tale." David Stuart Davies (ed.). *Children of the Night: Classic Vampire Stories*. London: Wordsworth Editions, 2007.

Rice, Anne. *The Vampire Lestat: Book II of The Vampire Chronicles*. New York: Ballantine Books, 1993.

Shakespeare, William. *Romeo and Juliet*. Brian Gibbons (ed.) London: Methuen Drama, 1980.

Shelley, Mary. *Frankenstein*. J. Paul Hunter (ed.) New York: W.W. Norton & Company, 1996.

Stoker, Bram. *Dracula*. Nina Auerbach and David J. Skal (eds.) London: W.W. Norton & Company, 1997.

Secondary Literature

Anderson, Richard. "*Dracula*, Monsters, and Apprehensions of Modernity." Carol Margaret Davison (ed.). *Bram Stoker's Dracula: Sucking through the Century 1897-1997*. Toronto; Oxford: Dundurn Press, 1997. 321-330.

Auerbach, Nina. *Our Vampires, Ourselves*. Chicago; London: University of Chicago Press, 1995.

Bell, Michael. *Sentimentalism, Ethics and the Culture of Feeling*. New York: Palgrave, 2000.

Beresford, Matthew. *From Demons to Dracula: The Creation of the Modern Vampire Myth*. London: Reaktion Books, 2008.

Binias, Silke. *Symbol and Symptom: the Femme Fatale in English poetry of the 19ᵗʰ century and feminist criticism*. Heidelberg: Winter Universitätsverlag, 2007.

Botting, Fred. *Gothic*. London; New York: Routledge, 2003.

Brittnacher, Hans Richard. *Ästhetik des Horrors: Gespenster, Vampire, Monster, Teufel und künstliche Menschen in der phantastischen Literatur*. Frankfurt am Main: Suhrkamp Verlag, 1994.

Broich, Ulrich and Manfred Pfister (eds.). *Intertextualität: Formen, Funktionen, anglistische Fallstudien*. Tübingen: Max Niemeyer Verlag, 1985.

Byron, Glennis. "'As one dead': *Romeo and Juliet* in the 'Twilight' zone." John Drakakis and Dale Townshend (eds.). *Gothic Shakespeares*. Abingdon; New York: Routledge, 2008. 167-185.

Carter, Margaret L. "The Vampire." S. T. Joshi (ed.). *Icons of Horror and the Supernatural: An Encyclopedia of Our Worst Nightmares, Volumes 1 and 2*. Westport, CT: Greenwood Press, 2007. 619-652.

Cochran, Kate. "'An Old-Fashioned Gentleman'? Edward's Imaginary History." Nancy R. Reagin (ed.). *Twilight & History*. New Jersey: John Wiley & Sons, Inc., 2010. 7-25.

Cohn, Dorrit. *Transparent Minds: Narrative Modes for Presenting Consciousness in Fiction*. Princeton, NJ: Princeton University Press, 1978.

Collings, Michael R, Dr. "Of Vampires and Their Ink: Traditions, Transformations, and the UnDead." George Beahm (ed.). *The Unauthorized Anne Rice Companion*. Kansas City, Mo.: Andrews and McMeel, 1996. 101-106.

Davis, Lloyd. "'Death-marked love': Desire and Presence in 'Romeo and Juliet'." Robert S. White (ed.). *Romeo and Juliet: Contemporary Critical Essays*. Basingstoke, Hampshire: Palgrave, 2001. 28-46.

Edwards, Kim. "Good Looks and Sex Symbols: The Power of the Gaze and the Displacement of the Erotic in *Twilight*." *Screen Education* 53 (2009): 26-32.

Ellis, Markman. *The History of Gothic Fiction*. Edinburgh: Edinburgh University Press, ³2005.

Fludernik, Monika. *Einführung in die Erzähltheorie*. Darmstadt: Wissenschaftliche Buchgesellschaft, 2006.

Frenzel, Elisabeth. *Stoff-, Motiv- und Symbolforschung*. Stuttgart: J. B. Metzler Verlag, ⁴1978.

Gassenmeier, Michael. *Der Typus des Man of Feeling: Studien zum sentimentalen Roman des 18. Jahrhunderts in England*. Tübingen: Max Niemeyer Verlag, 1972.

Gelder, Ken. *Reading the Vampire*. London; New York: Routledge, 1994.

Gordon, Joan and Veronica Hollinger (eds.). *Blood Read: The Vampire as Metaphor in Contemporary Culture.* Philadelphia: University of Pennsylvania Press, 1997.

Goetsch, Paul. *Monsters in English Literature: From the Romantic Age to the First World War.* Frankfurt am Main: Peter Lang, 2002.

Hallab, Mary Y. *Vampire God: The Allure of Undead in Western Culture.* New York: Suny Press, 2009.

Helbig, Jörg. *Intertextualität und Markierung: Untersuchungen zur Systematik und Funktion der Signalisierung von Intertextualität.* Heidelberg: Universitätsverlag C. Winter, 1996.

Hoffmeister, Gerhart. *Byron und der europäische Byronismus.* Darmstadt: Wissenschaftliche Buchgesellschaft, 1983.

Holland, Tom. "Undead Byron." Frances Wilson (ed.). *Byromania: Portraits of the Artist in Nineteenth- and Twentieth-Century Culture.* London: Macmillian Press, 1999. 154-165.

Hollinger, Veronica. "Fantasies of Absence: The Postmodern Vampire." Joan Gordon and Veronica Hollinger (eds.). *Blood Read: The Vampire as Metaphor in Contemporary Culture.* Philadelphia: University of Pennsylvania Press, 1997. 199-212.

Hogle, Jerrold E. *The Cambridge Companion to Gothic Fiction.* Cambridge: Cambridge University Press, 2002.

Housel, Rebecca and J. Jeremy Wisnewski (eds.). *Twilight and Philosophy: Vampires, Vegetarians and the Pursuit of Immortality.* Hoboken, NJ: John Wiley & Sons, Inc., 2009.

Hughes, William. "Fictional Vampires in the Nineteenth and Twentieth Centuries." David Punter (ed.). *A Companion to the Gothic.* Malden, Mass.: Blackwell Publishers Ltd., 2000. 143-154.

Klawitter, Arne and Michael Ostheimer. *Literaturtheorie - Ansätze und Anwendungen.* Göttingen: Vandenhoeck & Ruprecht, 2008.

Leatherdale, Clive. *Dracula - The Novel & the Legend: A Study of Bram Stoker's Gothic Masterpiece.* Brighton: Desert Island Books, [2]1993.

Locke, Andrea. "Immortal Fixation." *Theocrit: The Online Journal of Undergraduate Literary Criticism and Theory* 1.1 (Spring 2009): 62-68.

McGinley, Kathryn. "Development of the Byronic Vampire: Byron, Stoker, Rice." Gary Hoppenstand and Ray B. Browne (eds.). *The Gothic world of Anne Rice.* Bowling Green, OH: Bowling Green State University Popular Press, 1995. 71-90.

Mellor, Anne K. *Mary Shelley: Her Life, her Fiction, her Monsters.* New York, London: Routledge, 1989.

Mendoza, Stephanie. "From Dawn to Twilight: The Byronic Hero." *Theocrit: The Online Journal of Undergraduate Literary Criticism and Theory* 1.1 (Spring 2009): 9-24.

Moog-Grünewald, Maria. "Die Frau als Bild des Schicksals - Zur Ikonologie der Femme fatale." *Arcadia* 18.3 (1983): 240-257.

Müller, Wolfgang G. "Interfigurality: A Study of the Interdependence of Literary Figues." Heinrich F. Plett (ed.). *Intertextuality.* Berlin; New York: Walter de Gruyter, 1991. 101-121.

Mulvey-Roberts, Marie (ed.). *The Handbook to Gothic Literature.* New York: New York University Press, 1998.

Nelson, Gillian. "Vampiric Discourse in Emily Brontë's 'Wuthering Heights'." *Victorian Network* 1.1 (Summer 2009): 92-101.

Plett, Heinrich F. "Intertextualities." Heinrich F. Plett (ed.). *Intertextuality.* Berlin; New York: Walter de Gruyter, 1991. 3-29.

Pruckner, Chelsea. "Edward Cullen: The Phenomenon." *Ontologica: A Journal of Art and Thought* 1.1 (Summer 2009): 19-26.

Punter, David. *The Literature of Terror – A History of Gothic Fictions from 1765 to the present day. The Gothic Tradition, Volume I.* London; New York: Longman Group, ²1996.

---. *The Literature of Terror – A History of Gothic Fictions from 1765 to the present day. The Modern Gothic, Volume II.* London; New York: Longman Group, ²1996.

Pütz, Susanne. *Vampire und ihre Opfer: Der Blutsauger als literarische Figur.* Bielefeld: Aisthesis Verlag, 1992.

Ruthner, Clemens. *Am Rande: Kanon, Kulturökonomie und Intertextualität des Marginalen am Beispiel der (österreichischen) Phantastik im 20. Jahrhundert.* Tübingen: Francke, 2004.

Schneider, Jost. *Einführung in die Roman-Analyse.* Darmstadt: Wissenschaftliche Buchgesellschaft, 2003.

Stein, Atara. *The Byronic Hero in Film, Fiction, and Television.* Carbondale: Southern University Press, 2004.

Stanzel, Franz K. *Theorie des Erzählens.* Göttingen: Vandenhoeck und Ruprecht, ⁸2008.

---. *Typische Formen des Romans.* Göttingen: Vandenhoeck und Ruprecht, 1993.

Thöne, Leonie Viola. *Die Figur Edward Cullen: Moderner Mormonen-Missionar oder Vampir-Romantiker?* Dresden: edition Wissenschaft, 2009.

Thomalla, Ariane. *Die >femme fragile<: Ein literarischer Frauentypus der Jahrhundertwende.* Düsseldorf: Bertelsmann Universitätsverlag, 1972.

Todd, Janet. *Sensibility: An Introduction.* London; New York: Methuen & Co. Ltd., 1986.

Thorslev, Peter Larsen, Jr. *The Byronic Hero: Types and Prototypes.* Minneapolis: University of Minnesota Press, 1962.

Volkmer-Burwitz, Eva. *Tod und Transzendenz in der deutschen, englischen und amerikanischen Lyrik der Romantik und Spätromantik.* Frankfurt am Main: Peter Lang, 1987.

Wisker, Gina. "Love Bites: Contemporary Women's Vampire Fictions." David Punter (ed.). *A Companion to the Gothic.* Malden, Mass.: Blackwell Publishers Ltd., 2000. 167-179.

Internet Sources

Calchi Novati, Gabriella. "Who we might be – Performing the Potentialities of Otherness and Selfhood: Stephenie Meyer's Twilight Saga." *Inter-Disciplinary.Net: A Global Network for Dynamic Research and Publishing.* 2009. 1 Nov. 2010 <http://www.inter-disciplinary.net/wp-content/uploads/2009/08/g-calchi-novati-m7-draft-paper.pdf>.

Carter, Margaret L. "Revampings of Dracula in Contemporary Fiction." *Journal of Dracula Studies* Nr 3. 2001. 1 Nov. 2010 <http://blooferland.com/drc/images/03Carter.rtf>.

Cotsirilos, Teresa. "Bella and Byron: Stephenie Meyer's Twilight Series." *Harvard Book Review.* Volume XI, Number 1. 2010. 1 Nov. 2010 <http://www.hcs.harvard. edu/~hbr/main/current-issue/teresa-cotsirilos-bella-and-byron>.

Crossen, Carys. "'Would you please stop trying to take your clothes off?' Abstinence and Impotence of Male Vampires in Contemporary Horror Fiction and Film." *Inter-Disciplinary.Net: A Global Network for Dynamic Research and Publishing.* 2009. 1 Nov. 2010 <http://www.inter-disciplinary.net/wp-content/uploads/2009/08/crossen paper.pdf>.

Krishnan, Lakshmi. "'Why am I so changed?': Vampiric Selves and Gothic Doubleness in 'Wuthering Heights'." *Journal of Dracula Studies.* Nr 9. 2007. 1 Nov. 2010 <http://www.blooferland.com/drc/images/6/68/09Krishnan.rtf>.

Meyer, Stephenie. "Interview: 'Twilight' author Stephanie Meyer." Interview with Wm Morris. *A Motley Vision: Mormon Arts and Culture* 26.10.2005, 10.10.2010 <http://www.motleyvision.org/2005/interview-twilight-author-stephanie-meyer/>.

Meyer, Stephenie. "Love at First Bite: Stephenie Meyer talks about vampires, teen love, and her first novel, 'Twilight'." Interview with Rick Margolis. *School Library Journal* 1.10.2005, 3.6.2010 <http://www.schoollibraryjournal.com/article/CA6260602.html>.

Nelson, Elizabeth. "Monstrous Desire: Love, Death, and Marriage from Eros and Psyche to Edward and Bella." *Inter-Disciplinary.Net: A Global Network for Dynamic Research and Publishing.* 2009. 1 Nov. 2010 <http://www.inter-disciplinary.net/wp-content/uploads/2009/08/Nelson-paper.pdf >.

Stein, Atara. "Immortals and Vampires and Ghosts, Oh My!: Byronic Heroes in Popular Culture." *Romanticism and Contemporary Culture.* 2002. Romantic Circles. 12 pars. 1 Nov. 2010 <http://www.rc.umd.edu/praxis/contemporary/stein/stein.html>.

Stevens, Kirsten. "Meet the Cullens: Family, Romance and Female Agency in 'Buffy the Vampire Slayer' and 'Twilight'." *Slayage – The Journal of the Whedon Studies Association.* 8.1 [29] 64 pars. 1 Nov. 2010 <http://slayageonline.com/essays/ slayage29/Stevens.htm>.

The Official Website of Stephenie Meyer. Ed. Seth Meyer. 5 Oct. 2010. 1 Nov. 2010. <www.stepheniemeyer.com>.

Other Sources

New Moon – Biss zur Mittagsstunde. Dir. Chris Weitz. Perf. Kristen Stewart, Robert Pattinson, and Taylor Lautner. 2009. DVD. 2 Disc Fan Edition. Concorde Home Entertainment, 2010.

Rosemary's Baby. Dir. Roman Polanski. Perf. Mia Farrow, John Cassavetes, and Ruth Gordon. 1968. DVD. Paramount Pictures, 2001.

Twilight – Biss zum Morgengrauen. Dir. Catherine Hardwicke. Perf. Robert Pattinson, Kristen Stewart, and Billy Burke. 2008. DVD. 2 Disc Fan Edition. Concorde Home Entertainment, 2009.

9 783656 066248